Advance Praise for *Lead with Purpose*:

"The capacity to imagine and articulate exciting future possibilities is the defining competence of leaders. It's also the toughest of all skills for leaders to learn. That's what makes John Baldoni's new book, *Lead with Purpose*, so vitally important. It focuses on the one thing that makes leaders leaders—giving people a reason to believe and a reason to commit themselves to something meaningful and significant. This book is just a delight to read. John writes with elegance and ease about the solid evidence, valid principles, and practical ways in which real-life leaders bring purpose to life. I highly recommend that you make this one of your must-read books of the year."

> —**Jim Kouzes,** coauthor of the bestselling *The Leadership Challenge* and *The Truth About Leadership*; Dean's Executive Fellow of Leadership, Leavey School of Business, Santa Clara University

"*Lead with Purpose* inspires and instructs with research, interviews, stories, examples, reflective questions, lessons, and action steps."

> —**Dan McCarthy,** Director, Executive Education Programs, The Whittemore School of Business and Economics, University of New Hampshire

"Without a doubt, *Lead with Purpose* will help you reconnect to your own purpose and be a better leader for it."

> —**Ora Pescowitz, M.D.,** Executive Vice President for Medical Affairs, University of Michigan; CEO, U-M Health System

"Purpose drives passion and superior results. John Baldoni reminds us that meaning can be found in our work, no matter what it is we do. *Lead with Purpose* will change the way you lead for the better."

> —**Chester Elton,** bestselling author of *The Carrot Principle* and *The Orange Revolution*

"Anyone who wants to learn to lead effectively in this new era will be glad they made time to read *Lead with Purpose!*"

> —**Ari Weinzweig,** cofounder of Zingerman's, named "coolest company in America," *Inc.* magazine; author of *A Lapsed Anarchist's Approach to Building a Great Business*

LEAD WITH
PURPOSE

Giving Your Organization a Reason
to Believe in Itself

John Baldoni

AMACOM

American Management Association

New York • Atlanta • Brussels • Chicago • Mexico City • San Francisco
Shanghai • Tokyo • Toronto • Washington, D.C.

Bulk discounts available. For details visit:
www.amacombooks.org/go/specialsales
Or contact special sales:
Phone: 800-250-5308
E-mail: specialsls@amanet.org
View all the AMACOM titles at: www.amacombooks.org.

This publication is designed to provide accurate and authoritative information in regard to the subject matter covered. It is sold with the understanding that the publisher is not engaged in rendering legal, accounting, or other professional service. If legal advice or other expert assistance is required, the services of a competent professional person should be sought.

For portions of material used in the Action Planner, I am grateful to the following copyright owners for permission to adapt and use the following: Lesson 1. Action Steps adapted from John Baldoni, "A Better Kind of Leadership," December 19, 2007, FastCompany.com. Used with permission. Lesson 2. Action Steps adapted from John Baldoni, "Tune In or Forget It," October 31, 2007, FastCompany.com. Used with permission. Lesson 5. Action Steps adapted from John Baldoni, "Watch for the Reaction," November 7, 2007, FastCompany.com. Used with permission. Lesson 8. Sections on crafting your own story, reprinted from John Baldoni, "Craft a Narrative to Instill Optimism," Harvard Business Review (online), December 17, 2009. Used with permission.

Library of Congress Cataloging-in-Publication Data

Baldoni, John.
   Lead with purpose : giving your organization a reason to believe in itself / John Baldoni.
      p.   cm.
   Includes index.
   ISBN-13: 978-0-8144-1738-6
   ISBN-10: 0-8144-1738-8
   1. Leadership.   2. Employee motivation.   3. Organizational behavior.   I. Title.
HD57.7.B34894   2012
658.4'092—dc23

                                                              2011026463

About AMA

American Management Association (www.amanet.org) is a world leader in talent development, advancing the skills of individuals to drive business success. Our mission is to support the goals of individuals and organizations through a complete range of products and services, including classroom and virtual seminars, webcasts, webinars, podcasts, conferences, corporate and government solutions, business books, and research. AMA's approach to improving performance combines experiential learning—learning through doing—with opportunities for ongoing professional growth at every step of one's career journey.

Printing number

10   9   8   7   6   5   4   3   2   1

This book is dedicated to three exceptional individuals:

Dan Denison, who urged me to write about leadership

Marshall Goldsmith, who taught me to ask big questions

Michael Useem, who showed me that leadership
is a multidisciplinary adventure

CONTENTS

Contents

ACKNOWLEDGMENTS

The genesis of this book began with a lunch I had with participants of one of my workshops. The folks gathered at our table were talking about their expectations for work. None expected a lifetime contract from their employer, but based upon things they said I sensed that each of them had an expectation for doing work that meant something, that is, work that would make a positive difference in the lives of others.

Weeks later, when I was relating this conversation to my colleague Kathleen Macdonald, the concept of purpose in the workplace crystallized. As I thought about the role that purpose plays in the workplace and began researching the topic, I decided that it would make a good subject for a book. If employees are searching for meaning in work, whose job is it to find it for them? Must each employee find it for him- or herself? Or does it fall to the leader to provide purpose? And once found, how can leaders and followers put it to good use to achieve intended results? These are simple questions, but as I have learned they require thoughtful answers.

This book owes much to the men and women who are featured here. I call them my experts, and it is from them that many of the insights come. They are Dan Denison, Tom Draude, Tammy Erickson,

Marshall Goldsmith, Jim Guest, John Maxwell, Thomas Monahan, Vineet Nayar, George Reed, Michelle Rhee, Nancy Schlichting, Paul Spiegelman, Michael Useem, Roger Webb, and Pat Williams. Thank you, one and all.

Special thanks go to Barbara Allushuski, President of Right Management/Great Lakes Region, for helping me arrange some key interviews.

I also want to thank my editor at AMACOM, Christina Parisi, for believing in this book. The book neared completion just as Christina was delivering her third child; coincidentally, this is the second book of mine Christina has edited while with child. Her fortitude is inspirational.

Chuck Martin of NFI Research took my ideas for a survey and turned them into workable questions that generated meaningful results. I am grateful for Chuck's insights, as well as his patience. Thanks also go to Roger Kelleher of the American Management Association for enabling access to its database.

I am also indebted to Sarah McArthur and Kathryn Hyatt Stewart, who took the time to review the manuscript and provide insights that have made the book better. James Bessent supervised production and editing, and I thank him for his attentive patience with me.

Jeff Herman, my agent, deserves credit for pushing me to deliver a "next book" that would make a positive difference. I appreciate Jeff's advice and insights.

And, as ever, thanks go to the love of my life, Gail Campanella, my wife and soul mate.

LIST OF EXPERTS

The following were interviewed for their views on the role that purpose plays in creating and maintaining strong, healthy organizations.

- Dan Denison, Professor of Organization and Management, IMD Business School, Lausanne, Switzerland, and Founding Partner/CEO of Denison Consulting

- Retired Brigadier General Thomas V. Draude, President and Chief Executive Officer, Marine Corps University Foundation

- Tammy Erickson, consultant, McKinsey award–winning author, and named one of the 50 most influential living management thinkers by Thinkers 50

- Marshall Goldsmith, preeminent corporate executive coach and named by the American Management Association as one of the 50 great thinkers and business leaders who have impacted the field of management over the past 80 years

- Jim Guest, President and CEO, Consumers Union

- John Maxwell, Founder of the John Maxwell Company, and considered America's premier author on leadership

- Thomas Monahan, Chairman and CEO, The Corporate Executive Board

- Vineet Nayar, CEO, HCL Technologies

- George Reed, Professor of Leadership, University of San Diego, and retired Army Colonel

- Michelle Rhee, Founder and CEO, Students First, and former Chancellor of District of Columbia Public Schools

- Nancy Schlichting, CEO, Henry Ford Health System

- Paul Spiegelman, Founder/CEO, Beryl Companies

- Michael Useem, Professor of Management and Director of the Center for Change and Leadership, Wharton School, University of Pennsylvania

- Roger Webb, President, University of Central Oklahoma

- Pat Williams, Senior Vice President, Orlando Magic, and bestselling leadership and motivation author

A Note on the Research

In researching this book, I worked with NFI Research to find out how managers and employees viewed purpose and the role it plays within organizations. Using the database of the American Management Association, we surveyed 1,100 individuals. Results of the survey are integrated throughout the book as a means of underscoring key points.

The results from this study prove a salient point about leadership and management in the twenty-first century. People know the right things to do. As you will see from the data points cited at the end of relevant chapters, employees and managers have keen insight into how to promote purpose, not as some generic concept but in terms of specific suggestions. Many of these suggestions have been integrated into Action Steps that are itemized at the end of each chapter and fleshed out more fully in the Action Planner.

It is my belief that readers will find these suggestions to be worthy of consideration and, taken in conjunction with the opinions quoted by experts throughout the book, a firm foundation based in real-world practice that will help managers and employees alike not only find purpose within their organizations, but also to act upon it to achieve intended results.

●　　●　　●　　●　　●　　●　　●

Note: The entire report is contained in the Appendix.

LEAD WITH PURPOSE

PROLOGUE

> Very little is needed to make a happy life. It is all within
> yourself, in your way of thinking.
>
> —MARCUS AURELIUS

When organizations succeed, it is because they know *what* they do and *why* they do it. We say they have "purpose."

Let me share a story. Not long ago I walked into an Apple store to inquire when the company might be introducing an external keyboard for the iPhone. The young man who handled my query was polite, but direct, "We are committed to the onscreen keyboard." Note the word "we." How many times have you heard a clerk in a store refer to the business as "we," in particular to a customer who wants something the store does not carry? While some might have thought the young man arrogant, I did not. I considered him committed. His demeanor demonstrated that he believed in Apple, its product line, and its organizational purpose. This young man was acting on purpose, for purpose, and with purpose.

When I share this story with senior executives, I ask them: What would you give to have an entire company full of employees like the young man who assisted me? They smile wistfully, knowing that such commitment is rare. But in reality, it is only rare because companies do not take enough time to nurture such purposeful attitudes and results in the workplace.

It is up to leaders to make certain that organizational purpose is understood and acted upon. Based upon research and interviews with business executives in multiple sectors, I have concluded that there are seven key people-smart things that organizations must do to succeed in the new future.

1. **Make purpose a central focus.** Organizations that succeed are those that know where they are headed and why. It is up to leaders to use that sense of purpose to shape the destiny of their organizations and leverage the talents of the people in them to achieve intended results.

2. **Instill purpose in others.** While it may be a cliché to say that "people matter," reality dictates that they do indeed matter. It is important to teach purpose to your people so that they have a sense of what the organization does and the role they play in it.

3. **Make employees comfortable with ambiguity.** The world as we knew it at the beginning of the century is over and it is never coming back. With this new reality comes a sense of unease. We had grown accustomed to growth as a universal right. No longer will that be true. What will be true however is that purpose can provide clarity in unsettled times. Having strong purpose can provide the direction that employees need to navigate through ambiguity.

4. **Turn good intentions into great results.** The world is tough and people matter, but you still have to get the work done. Purpose can be an enabling factor that provides the link people need to connect what they do to what the organization needs them to do. When

that happens, employees can turn ideas into practical applications that satisfy customer needs.

5. **Make it safe to fail (as well as prevail).** Purpose is the engine of innovation. While innovation relies upon creativity for spark, it is purpose that turns ideas into practical concepts. No company will succeed all of the time, but it needs to allow its work force to think and act creatively (and occasionally fail) as a means of preparing the organization to meet new and emerging challenges.

6. **Develop the next generation.** Few senior executives will be in their current jobs in five or ten years from now. They may be heading other organizations or they may have retired. Savvy organizations are purposeful about how they develop future leaders. They integrate leadership development into how they run their operations.

7. **Prepare yourself.** Purposeful organizations need leaders who know themselves first; that is, they have an inner compass that points them in the right direction. Such leaders catalyze their own purpose to help their organizations succeed.

This is not by any means an exclusive list of factors affecting people-smart development. In fact, it is only a starting point. The final chapter of this book will explore how leaders can begin to think about, identify, and ultimately learn to cope or take advantage of the factors shaping their own businesses with regard to their own people development.

Purpose can be a driving force for an organization to achieve its intended results. Purpose forms the backbone of what an organization exists to do; upon which you can build vision and mission. A central challenge for leaders is to bring people together for common cause.

That's purpose. Purpose is the why behind everything within an organization.

This book will show how leaders can unlock the purpose of their organizations and put it to good use for employees to apply to their own jobs. The net effect is to help individuals, teams, and organizations to optimize performance by understanding how to use purpose for good intention.

Leveraging Lessons to Meet Future Challenges

Leaders use purpose to build strong organizations. Importantly, leaders also challenge themselves as well as their employees to lead with, for, and on purpose. That becomes possible because purposeful people have an inner strength that we sometimes overlook: an ability to adapt. Yes, change can be hard, even painful, but executives are among the most capable and resourceful people on the planet. The ideas developed in this book will provide leaders with an approach and a methodology to leverage purpose that is robust, vibrant, and most of all, flexible and resilient.

How well leaders use purpose to create the vision, mold the mission, and shape the values will serve as a testament to their ability to bring people together for common cause. All of us cherish the opportunity to participate in endeavors that engage our intellect, capture our hearts, and enrich our spirits. Purpose can be the great enabler that links leaders and followers together in order to make a positive difference in their organizations.

It is important for business and public sector leaders to understand their responsibility to instill purpose in the workplace in order to harness the talents of their people. Not only will they succeed in the present but they will also prevail for generations to come.

Purpose matters.

CHAPTER 1

LEAD FOR PURPOSE

> "I like to see a man proud of the place in which he lives.
> I like to see a man live in it so that his place will be
> proud of him."
>
> —ABRAHAM LINCOLN

The mood in the room seemed to match the mood outside; it was a cold and overcast October morning. Talk was subdued and dark humor prevailed. The managers had gathered for a scenario planning session that I was helping to facilitate, but it was easy to tell that their minds were elsewhere. The media were reporting that this company was about to be bought by a competitor, so many in the room were feeling that any talk about the future, let alone talk of today, was moot.

The mood changed as soon as their boss, a vice president, rose to speak. He addressed the issue of the day and said that he had no further information to share. But he sympathized with how people were feeling, and he offered to meet with them and their teams anytime they asked. He then challenged the group to focus on why they had gathered. He wanted them to shift from thinking about what they could not do to what they could do. Right now, that thinking was to focus on the immediate future.

The vice president did what all good leaders facing a crisis, or any serious problem, must do: Give the group a reason to believe. He did not dispense false hope, but he gave them something more powerful: purpose. When a group has purpose, its members will work together; they will pull together to make things happen. Purpose is the guiding beacon of every successful organization.

• • • • • • •

The beauty of the American management model is that it is based on action. That is why the model is emulated throughout the world: Americans know how to get things done. But sometimes getting things done happens at the expense of forethought. In their book *The India Way*, the authors, two Americans and two Indians, discuss one of the pillars of the Indian way that they label "holistic employee engagement."[1] Central to engagement is purpose: People have to know what they are doing and why they are being asked to do it.

How to Discover Organizational Purpose

Purpose shapes vision, which, quite simply, is where you want to go. *Vision* is the lodestar that shines in the distance and serves as a guiding light. Vision is the process of becoming; organizationally, it is like saying what you want to be when you grow up. Very often, vision opens with an infinitive verb: *to be*. This is expressed as "to be number one," "to be the most respected," "to be the one of choice," and so on. It is aspirational in nature.

Mission is what the organization does. It is purpose expressed as action. It is the what, why, and how of an organization: what it does, why it does it, and how it does it. For example, a mission statement for a bakery might focus on making bread and pastries with high-quality ingredients in an artisan style for customers seeking authentic flavor. Reading this statement, you discern purpose.

Values are what hold people together. They embody the beliefs by which people in the organization choose to abide. Take a hospital. Its values define the respect that employees must manifest toward patients as well as toward each other. Words like *dignity, ethics,* and *respect* are prevalent. Values, when they are implemented, become measures by which people hold each other accountable. The end of this chapter contains a guide to defining purpose.

Taken together, vision, mission, and values underscore the culture, the glue of an organization. While the concept of culture is broad and deep, when it comes to purpose, we can be very direct and to the point. Quite simply, *culture* is what the employees perceive as reality inside their organizations. It can be open, tolerant, and flexible, or it can be closed, intolerant, and rigid. Culture does not depend on purpose, but it is greatly influenced by it. Open cultures nurture purpose as if it were mutable and alive; closed cultures regard it as defined and inorganic.

Along with culture, corporate vision, mission, and values are essential to framing purpose, but they are only a starting point. Employees need to internalize them so that they are relevant. Something can become relevant only if it is understood, and that is where the manager comes into play. It falls to the manager to make the culture real. How he or she does this is central to the concept of purpose.

So, how does a manager make purpose relevant? Link it to the work! For some organizations, such as the bakery just mentioned, this is easy. Make the dough, bake the goods, sell to customers, and watch them come back for more. Okay, how do you make purpose relevant if you are the distribution manager for a pipe supply company? You work with spreadsheets and you field phone calls from internal and external customers. How do you discuss purpose? You explain to your employees that logistics are the linchpin of the pipe supply operation. If distribution does not gather and warehouse pipe products from the factory or other sources, you have nothing to sell. If you cannot identify and ship products in a timely fashion, customers cannot buy. How you iterate this is critical to purpose.

Expression of purpose may begin with words—chiefly, explanations of what the organization does and why it does it. But words go only so far. Purpose, if it is to be sustainable, must be linked to organizational culture and values. That is vital. Here are some ways to reinforce this connection.

"Purpose comes down to having clear-cut, definite goals," says Pat Williams, bestselling leadership author. "They are powerful motivating forces. Those goals have to be out in front of the organization. They've got to be written down [as well as] reminded and reviewed." Regarding the Orlando Magic, the NBA team where Williams serves as a senior vice president, "We talk about two things all the time: winning a championship and keeping every seat full. No one in the organization can miss that."[2]

Putting people first, says Michelle Rhee, onetime chancellor of the Washington, D.C., school district, "is about creating a culture that constantly recognizes people for the work they're doing." That requires the involvement of a leader who "ensures that people's voices are heard."[3]

Purpose in education is a straightforward proposition for Rhee. It stems from doing "what's right and good for kids." It was a mantra she took personally and one that she preached throughout the community. That kind of clarity is something that every leader in any field should strive to drive throughout their organization. Reducing purpose to a simple statement is not easy, but it can be a valuable tool in clarifying intention for employees.

While working in another job prior to running the D.C. school district, Rhee learned that creating the right culture depends on doing the little things that matter to people—for example, being accessible to the CEO. It is important, says Rhee, that people have a voice with the leader at the top. "I think oftentimes it's the smaller things that feel more personalized that make people feel valued and recognized."[4] When serving as chancellor of the school district, Rhee made a habit of reaching out regularly to all levels of the organization. She would personally call a principal or a teacher and thank the individual for the good work he or she was doing.

Dangers of Having No Purpose

Purpose may seem elusive, and it may be tempting to abandon the concept altogether, but consider the alternative: lack of purpose. This leads to organizational listlessness. People may be doing their individual jobs appropriately, but soon each will come to the realization that individual contributions are good, but not great. What is necessary is to get people to pull together for the common cause.

"I don't think you can hit purpose enough as a senior leader," says George Reed, a retired Army colonel who consults in the corporate sector. "It is one of those things that can be undercommunicated by an order of magnitude. You cannot oversell, overpronounce 'Here's why we're here.'" If purpose is not communicated, Reed believes, it will be lost in the "urgencies of the day" that cause people to forget their original intentions and their passion. "The senior leader who bangs that drum, who serves as the symbolic voice of the organization . . . reminds their people that what they're doing is important."[5]

Leaders Drive Purpose

It falls to the leader to ensure that employees know what makes the organization tick. Only a leader who knows him- or herself can do this effectively. Consider what your own purpose is. One question that I often use in my executive coaching is a time-honored one: *What gets you up in the morning?*

So often this question serves as an icebreaker. I have seen an executive's eyes light up when asked. It gives the individual the opportunity to talk about what he or she likes to do and why. Many of the folks I have the privilege of coaching become very animated telling me about what excites them about their work. For many, it is the opportunity to do what they have always wanted to do. Engineers love solving problems, so that's a common response. Finance people talk about the joy of a disciplined balance sheet. Senior managers speak about the satisfaction they feel at seeing all the parts of an organization functioning in harmony.

What these folks are addressing is individual purpose. In organizations, leaders define the meaning of *purpose* as "doing something for others." Here are two questions leaders can use to clarify purpose:

1. **Why does my team need to know about purpose?** This is the number one question. You need to answer it for yourself first and

then explain it to your team. For example, if you are in finance, what makes your work purposeful? This becomes an opportunity to link your team's functional expertise. You are responsible for maintaining cash flow as well as providing guidance for planning decisions. How you explain that to your team will go a long way toward their understanding the implications of their work.

2. **How can I make purpose more relevant to my team?** Your team is looking to you for answers, so you need to make purpose explicit. The easy way to do this is to explain how the work your team does contributes to the smooth running of the organization. A better way is to tell stories about the work. Consider how your customers judge your work. You likely have examples of success that are worth sharing. Returning to our finance example, talk about how one of your colleagues complimented your team on making the budgeting process easier to understand, allowing him to complete the planning process in a more timely fashion.

These two questions quantify the role a leader plays in determining the purpose and meaning of work for the team. Many people, however, are searching for deeper meaning, satisfaction, enrichment, and happiness. While these may be existential issues, answers can be found in purposeful work. Let's take them one at a time.

Meaning

We want to know that our work matters to others—customers, colleagues, and managers. Consider meaning as the substance of what we do that has an impact on others. One thought that kept Viktor Frankl, a Jewish psychiatrist imprisoned by the Nazis in a concentration camp, alive was his desire to see his life's work published on a form of therapy he called logotherapy. This determination forms the background of his book, *Man's Search for Meaning*, which chronicles his quest to ensure that extreme deprivation, suffering, and violence suffered by inmates such as himself had meaning.[6]

Satisfaction

Compensation provides the floorboard for job satisfaction. In October 2009, a study by McKinsey & Company revealed that six in ten employees regarded performance-based compensation as "extremely" or "very" effective. Just over 50 percent said that increases in base pay were as effective.[7] (Only 35% found stock or stock options effective. People seem to want real money, not "maybe money.")

As it relates to purpose, managers need to find ways to compensate their team fairly. Research has consistently shown that money is more of a satisfier than a motivator. Too little compensation is a demotivator, but lots of money does not ensure higher levels of engagement or effort.

Enrichment

Finding proper ways to motivate your team is essential, but so often managers forget that what people really want is recognition. This same McKinsey & Company study showed that the satisfaction employees seek from their jobs is more than just money. Two-thirds surveyed said that "praise and commendation from an immediate manager" was extremely effective, and over 60 percent said that "attention from leaders" was also effective. Buttressing the data is the fact that 62 percent surveyed said that a strong motivator was "opportunities to lead projects or task forces."[8] Compensation is essential, but emotional satisfiers are more rewarding.

The upshot of these findings is that managers need to find ways to recognize their employees' contributions. As regards purpose, it falls to managers to allow their people more opportunities to lead by delegating not simply responsibility but also authority. Those who accept the challenge and prove themselves are the future leaders of the organization.

Happiness

Researchers believe that emotions, particularly happiness, can be the result of the collective condition of people around you. "Your happiness depends not just on your choices and actions, but also on the choices and actions of people you don't even know who are one, two and three degrees removed from you," said Dr. Nicholas A. Christakis, a physician and social scientist at Harvard Medical School. "Emotions have a collective existence—they are not just an individual phenomenon." These conclusions result from a study coauthored by Dr. Christakis and James Fowler that analyzed the happiness levels of over 4,700 participants in the famous Framingham heart study.[9]

The implications for managers are clear. Managers can have an effect on how their employees feel at work. Most important, it falls to them to create conditions where employees can succeed. Managers do this by providing training and resources for employees to do their jobs, along with adequate time to do the work. Experience tells us that time and resources are often in short supply, but managers can help overcome such shortages through open and honest communication: Tell employees what they have to work with and how long they have to complete the job. Setting realistic expectations is essential.

How a manager communicates is critical to employee happiness. When conditions are tough, managers should be realistic but resolve to spread good cheer. Talk about what employees are working on and how well you regard each employee's contribution. Help each person understand his or her particular role. Managers who are in the habit of looking at the bright side will position work as something positive. Likewise, happiness reinforces a sense of purpose because people like coming to work, want to be with their colleagues, and aspire to do a good job. It makes them feel good.

How to Instill Purpose at Work

Mission is essential to accountability, says Jim Guest, President and CEO of Consumers Union. "It helps to be working for a mission-driven organization where people can really embrace and take great pride and satisfaction in the mission and what they are doing to advance it." Guest adds, "We really do feel we're working to make society better, or to make people's lives better." For Guest, accountability depends on being trustworthy. His commitment to the organization is, as he says, in his DNA. "I believe in being open and honest."[10] As a colleague puts it, "Jim rolls up his sleeves"; he is transparent because people can see exactly what he is up to. This fosters a high degree of trust as well as followership.

"Trust is something that doesn't happen overnight," says Roger Webb, President of the University of Central Oklahoma (UCO). "You can't make a good speech and greet your employees and all of a sudden [have them] trust you." Webb likens trust to building a bank account that you accumulate over time. It is important for a leader to show vulnerability at the same time: "You have to fight for them and appreciate their support in return."[11]

Values augment the trust equation. At UCO, they're called the three Cs: character, commitment, and community. Faculty members in all disciplines are expected to find ways to talk about these values. Webb himself teaches a freshman leadership class. Students are expected to integrate these values into their lives. UCO gives scholarships to incoming students who have exhibited leadership in high school, either at school, in an extracurricular activity, or in their community. UCO is a service-oriented university focused on producing educated men and women who remain in the state and contribute to their communities through civic activities.

"Leaders can make people feel comfortable if they develop trust . . . that's the most important quality in business," says Paul Spiegelman, founder and CEO of the Beryl Companies, a call center business specializing in healthcare based in Texas. Leaders demonstrate trust when it matters most. During the Great Recession, when many companies were eliminating 401(k) contributions, Beryl Companies doubled theirs. "I want people to thank me when they're sixty-five," jokes Spiegelman. But turning serious, he adds that such measures "create loyalty and that's what creates trust."[12]

People building a business need to decide whether they are in it for the short term or the long term, says Dan Denison, professor of management at IMD business school in Lausanne, Switzerland. The way to sustain growth over time "is through the next person they hire."[13] If that employee is developed in the right way, he or she will come to embody the organization's DNA.

Denison knows something about building a business, since he is the founding partner and CEO of Denison Consulting. Together with colleague Bill Neale, Denison developed the Denison Organizational Culture Survey, a leading instrument for assessing organizational health and effectiveness.[14] "The main thing you learn from managing a firm that I didn't understand as an academic is that you speak through your actions." Executives can craft expert messages, but in times of uncertainty, employees look to their leader for more than words. They look for reassurance. Employees, says Denison, have a perennial question: "What about me?"[15]

Let People Know They Matter

"Demonstrate through your actions that people come first," says Nancy Schlichting, CEO of the Henry Ford Health System, located in southeast Michigan. Given the economic hardship the region has endured in the first decade of the twenty-first century, the Henry Ford Health System has cut costs severely. One thing it did not cut was training and development. "It sent a message to our people that we were serious about our commitment to people," reports Schlichting.[16]

For Schlichting, investment in people is only part of the equation. She makes herself available to anyone in the health system, saying, "People in our organization have complete access to me." Sometimes that involves helping an employee's child find a job in the health system, or even airing an issue with a supervisor. "I don't interfere with the normal chain of command and people don't abuse it." Schlichting's example sets the tone for managers throughout the system. "I don't solve problems I shouldn't solve," she emphasizes, though at the same time, she expects managers throughout the system to be available to their employees. That affirms the "people first" equation that radiates throughout Henry Ford.[17]

Putting people first, according to Paul Spiegelman of the Beryl Companies, comes down to a belief in people. Spiegelman says you need to believe that people do come first and then you have to show this, first with words: "You've got to say it, say it often, and in multiple different ways." Backing words with actions is essential; doing right by your people. Purpose then comes together by demonstrating to your employees that you care about them, and they in turn reflect that care to their customers by delivering superior service. As Spiegelman says, "There is a link between building a people-focused organization and driving better outcomes and results for your customers."[18]

Call center work is less than glamorous, yet it is vitally important to patient care. As Spiegelman explains, "We connect people to health care by making appointments with physicians, signing people up for community education programs, and making post-discharge calls to patients." To work effectively, call center employees need to understand how their work "can improve the patient experience outside the four walls of the hospital."[19]

Linking purpose to results through employee engagement is something of a calling for Spiegelman. In 2007, he wrote *Why Is Everyone Smiling?*, a book about his experiences as CEO and the fundamental role culture plays at Beryl. He then teamed with author Bo Burlingham to cofound the Small Giants Community, a nonprofit organization dedicated to helping small businesses network to learn from and share best practices related to leveraging the importance of meaning in the workplace.[20]

Reach Out to Employees as Individuals

When Jim Guest arrived at Consumers Union as its CEO, he made a habit of introducing himself to employees. "I would just drop into people's offices, total strangers, and say 'Hey, what are you up to? What are you working on? What's your job?'" Word soon got around that Guest was truly curious as well as genuinely interested in what employees did and how they did it.

Guest continues the practice today by eating in the cafeteria with employees. "I'll make it a point to sit down at different tables. I often sit with people I don't even know . . . and just talk to them." For Guest, such exchanges yield insights into what is really going on in his organization. "I often learn more from [conversations with employees] than I do from reports I get." Guest also makes certain that new employees know that his door is open to them. He tells them "feel free to stop me in the hall or to make an appointment and come to my office." True enough, not many do make those appointments, but Guest says, "I do get stopped in the hall." Sometimes Guest will turn those impromptu chats into immediate invitations to his office. This is important to employees. As Guest says, "It's easy to forget how much a small interaction with a chief executive can be so meaningful to people."[21]

Communication is important to Guest's leadership style. Prior to making decisions, he says, "I'm not looking for a consensus, but I am looking to consult or to gather information from people." Communicating as he does with people at all levels in the company gives Guest a good sense of what's going on in the organization.[22]

Communications and Behavior

"The best form of communication is example," says Tom Draude, President and CEO of the Marine Corps University Foundation and a retired Marine brigadier general. One story that brings this notion of example setting into sharp focus is from Draude's experience in Vietnam, where he served three tours of duty. Once as a Marine captain, his rifle company endeavored to take a heavily fortified hamlet. Artillery and air support could not dislodge the enemy so Draude decided to take his team in. The resulting attack resulted in the death of a young corporal, Fred Miller. As Draude explains, Miller's body was outside the lines and so he went to retrieve it.

The next day, the battalion commander arrived and asked about the blood on Draude's flak jacket; when he learned about Draude's retrieval mission, he went ballistic. Draude replied, "Sir, I understand what you are saying but you must understand that if it happened again I'd do the same thing because I'll never leave behind the body of a dead or wounded Marine."[23] Draude recalls thinking that his career was about to end very quickly, especially when the assistant division commander of First Marine Division arrived on the scene. The general asked who was in charge, and when Draude spoke up, the general "grabs my hand and starts pumping away slapping me on the back and saying, 'God, that was great, Captain. That was super. That's what we're looking for.'" Then the general turned to the battalion commander, knowing nothing of the reprimand, and said, "Colonel, with company commanders like this, how can you go wrong?"[24]

Draude, who would one day serve as Assistant Division Commander in Operation Desert Storm, recalls that his action to retrieve Corporal Miller's body was not done to show his men that they wouldn't be left behind. Nonetheless, "that example certainly demonstrated to them that I cared about my people and the fact that they were important and are still important to me." In retrospect, Draude says, "it was a lot harder to confront my battalion commander than it was to lead a bayonet assault." The latter required physical courage, while the former required a willingness to speak truth to power.[25]

After thirty years in the Marines, Draude became an executive with USAA, a financial services and insurance company for active military and veterans. He made it a habit of showing up when the workload was heavy and employees had to work weekends. Some would ask him why he was there. "Because you're here," he'd reply. Draude was not there to supervise, because he trusted his employees as experts in their jobs. By way of explanation, Draude adds wryly, "The most dangerous thing on a submarine is an officer with a screwdriver." Turning serious, he notes, "You dignify what [employees] do by your presence." At USAA, "we had a saying, 'You can pretend to care but you cannot pretend to be there.' There is no substitute for demonstrating your commitment that is as strong as just showing up."[26]

For Draude, presence means walking around and knowing employees by name. At USAA, he would make a point of talking to employees about their families, even noting the pictures of people that employees had posted in their cubicles and asking questions about them. Draude notes that these are small gestures, but "these are the things important to employees and they are right out there for you. All you have to do is be smart enough to observe." That is what good leaders do as a means of connecting with their people. "You can't fake sincerity, but if you sincerely care about your people you demonstrate it by knowing their names, showing up [where they work], and demonstrating a genuine interest in them," Draude concludes.[27]

Instilling purpose comes from matching what the organization stands for with what it strives to achieve. Driving that sense of purpose home to individuals within the organization is a challenge that every leader faces.

Defining Purpose

Defining purpose is a straightforward proposition. In its simplest form, purpose is the organization's reason for being. It is a combination of vision, mission, and values.

To define an organization's purpose, you must ask three questions:

1. What is our vision—that is, what do we want to become?
2. What is our mission—that is, what do we do now?
3. What are our values—that is, what are the behaviors we expect of ourselves?

Answers to these questions will provoke thinking and discussion. Defining purpose, if it does not already exist, is an exercise in leadership. It is a means by which an organization comes to grips with how it sees itself.

True purpose does not exist in a vacuum. It must be put to good use. Leaders communicate it as a means to fulfilling an organization's vision, mission, and values. It also points people in the right direction so that they can achieve results for the organization, for the team, and for themselves.

Lead for Purpose: Survey Results

We surveyed over 1,100 employees and managers to get their ideas on the importance of purpose in the workplace. Their responses have been integrated into the end of every chapter as a means of amplifying and illustrating key points. Some of what they told us has also been turned into the suggested Action Steps for implementing purpose, and those suggestions are found in each chapter as well as in the Action Planner. Full survey results can be found in the Appendix.

What Employees and Managers Say

Over 90 percent of those surveyed believed that leaders instill purpose in the workplace by:

- Communicating the vision
- Linking work to results
- Showing how customers benefit from what employees do
- Doing what they promise
- Instilling confidence

Two-thirds of respondents believed that leaders could instill purpose using merit pay.

What Leaders Must Do

Organizational purpose must be clear, and it is up to leaders to make it so. They must sharpen the focus to make the vision clear. One way to do this is to communicate the purpose regularly, but also to link the vision to the mission and, by extension, to results. A good way to do this is to enable employees to see the fruits of their labors—that is, let them know how their products and services impact the lives of customers.

Setting the right example and living up to it reinforces a leader's authority and ability. Employees want to know that those in charge do what is asked of them—and more. Leaders must also radiate confidence; employees like to know that their leaders are up to the task.

How to Lead for Purpose

Leadership Questions

- How well have I taught purpose to my team?
- What can I do to instill clarity of purpose to my team?

Leadership Directives

- Describe the purpose of your organization in a single sentence; for example, "We make great cars and trucks"; "We deliver compassionate care to seniors"; "We provide training for adults seeking second careers"; "We make great food for a great low price."

- Make it clear that employees who know the organization's purpose can do their jobs with a greater sense of awareness of their own contributions.

- Link employee engagement to organizational effectiveness—that is, people matter.

- Demonstrate how you find meaning in your own work. Tell stories about your sources of inspiration.

- Challenge employees to find purpose in their own work. Ask managers to discuss purpose regularly at staff meetings.

- Live the values of the organization. Abide by your principles. Stand up for what is right.

CHAPTER 2

INSPIRE PURPOSEFUL PEOPLE

"Thinking too well of people often allows them to be better
than they otherwise would."

—NELSON MANDELA, FORMER SOUTH AFRICAN PRESIDENT

For 27 years, Nelson Mandela was cut off from his family and
friends and was imprisoned on a barren island off the coast of
South Africa. Labeled a terrorist and condemned to a life sentence,
Mandela fought the temptation to hate his enemy and instead sought
to understand more about him. He even learned the language of his
oppressor, Afrikaans.

It turned out to be good preparation, for after he was released
from prison in 1990 and the apartheid era came to an end, Mandela
was elected president in the country's first fair and free election in
1994. Mandela used the opportunity not to dish out punishment to
those who had wronged him but, rather like Abraham Lincoln, to
"bind up the wounds" of his divided country and seek the establishment of a new culture for South Africa.[1]

Mandela was a leader who believed in the innate goodness of people. Early in his presidency he used the opportunity of the staging of the 1995 Rugby World Cup in Johannesburg as an attempt to bring peace. Rugby was a game favored by whites, not blacks, but Mandela worked to bring the races together harmoniously by uniting them toward a single goal: winning the World Cup for South Africa. This story is told in the book *Playing the Enemy,* by John Carlin. Mandela told Carlin that he wanted to use sport as a means of nation building. In his first meeting with Francois Pienaar, captain of the South African rugby team, Mandela expressed his idea that sports, particularly this rugby tournament, could be a means by which people could put aside past prejudice in order to forge a new national identity. A bold notion certainly, but as Carlin explains, Pienaar left this meeting with Mandela certain that he had the president's support as well as his friendship.[2] Encouraging people to believe in themselves so that the organization can achieve is a noble quest, requiring a leader who can not only see beyond the horizon but also make what is over that horizon tangible for others and even attainable. Organizational theorists call this "transformational leadership."

●　　●　　●　　●　　●　　●　　●

Transformational leadership rests, as it did for Mandela, on instilling purpose in people by treating them as contributors rather than as adversaries. Mandela did it by putting aside any bitterness he had developed as a black man living under the oppression of apartheid and reaching out to whites and blacks to create a new society that would allow the races to live in harmony.

Few leaders will face the obstacles to unity that Mandela did, but every leader will find him- or herself facing challenges that can be solved only by finding ways to bring people together for a common purpose. This can be accomplished only by connecting with people in ways that affirm their dignity and confirm the need for their participation in the work the organization does.

Marshall Goldsmith, long considered the nation's preeminent executive coach, says, "The way leaders can demonstrate that they put people first is, rather than telling people what to do and how to do it, instead ask for their input, listen to their ideas, and learn from them. Then demonstrate this learning through ongoing follow-up and actions that show they are indeed putting people first."[3]

"If leaders don't believe there's purpose, they can't instill it," says Nancy Schlichting of Henry Ford Health System. Leaders need to imbue their organizations with a sense of purpose, and they do this through words and actions. Part of communicating purpose is demonstrating the possibilities that come with the job. As Schlichting says, "We have to be able to convey it in a way that really helps others step back from the day-to-day grind and really understand that they have a unique opportunity."[4]

Making Tough Decisions

When a company lays off employees but its senior managers get rewarded through bonuses, "it erodes trust," says Schlichting. Where tight times at her company have meant *no* salary increases, leadership was not exempt. Acting in this manner struck "a chord of credibility and trust," says Schlichting. "We did it with the clear explanation that we would save hundreds of jobs each year. Everyone in this community understands that job loss is the worst thing they can get." Employees understood, and as Schlichting explains, employee engagement scores actually went up. The health system is regularly recognized as one of the best places to work in southeast Michigan.[5]

"The concept we always used in the military was 'mission first, people always,'" says George Reed, professor of leadership at the University of San Diego, California. Yet in times of war, it is true that all soldiers will not return home safely. Therefore, there is a shift of emphasis from individuals to organization, explains Reed, who is also a retired Army colonel. "It's not about me; it's about we. It's not a universal statement that people come first. It's the purpose of the organization that comes first."[6]

"The best leaders exist to serve their organizations," says Reed. He recalls the example of his favorite leader in the military. The man would say, "Look, folks, I don't know more about what it is we're supposed to be doing here than you do. You know more about that than I do. But what I want to do is help you. And I'm going to help you by asking hard questions and by suggesting alternative approaches." In this way, service to the organization manifests itself as service to individuals.[7]

Tom Monahan, CEO of Corporate Executive Board, believes that leaders on the whole do not do a good enough job of "connecting the dots" between mission and outcome. Executives in his firm try to show how the impact of what they do affects the careers of the clients they serve. "We spend time helping people understand how what they do [supports the mission]." Monahan feels pride when clients "retired from a role and looked back on their careers and reflected on how, in their hardest times, we helped them be successful."[8]

Corporate Executive Board sponsors a class it calls "Center of the Enterprise," in which employees learn how values, mission, and strategies are interconnected. "Values," Monahan believes, "connect to the business outcomes we care about."[9] It requires effort, but it is something in which Monahan and his leadership team invest themselves fully.

For Roger Webb, at UCO, understanding a sense of purpose is essential for dealing with tough times. Like many universities that receive funding from the state, his has had to cut expenditures and trim head count. "If people don't feel the purpose and don't feel the goal and feel like they're accomplishing things and moving forward, then depressing news can really bring people down," says Webb. Living with the status quo is not an option; you need to motivate and inspire employees. According to Webb, that comes from demonstrating through actions that employees' contributions do matter.[10]

The Role of a Leader-Manager

One way leaders can connect effectively with their people is to understand the value of work, not by simply quantifying it in terms of dollars and cents but also in recognizing its strategic importance. It is tempting to quantify people's work in terms of an organizational chart, but that tells you only who is responsible, not who actually does the work. They may not be one and the same. Therefore, there are three questions a manager can ask:

1. **What is the work?** Work is anything an employee does to add value to the organization, whether it is creating a report full of statistics and projections, or stapling that report together for distribution to senior management. Work is work. But all jobs are not equal, and, therefore, it falls to the manager to decide who does what.

2. **Who does the work?** A great deal of work is tactical. It is the day-to-day things we do to keep a business humming or a nonprofit

serving its constituents. Identifying who should do what is a manager's responsibility. It is important to assign people to tasks they can do well and that are best suited to their skills. Easy to say, but so often employees are in the wrong slots. Some highly trained folks are doing work that could be done by entry-level employees, or frontline employees are challenged to do more than they are equipped to do. Sometimes frontline managers spend too much time working beneath them; that is, they are too involved in details when they should be thinking of ways to let their direct reports do the work.

3. **How does the work get done?** We all want the idealized workflow: just enough to keep us busy but not too much to overwhelm us. But all too often, especially in times of scarcity, most of us are working over capacity. We are stretched to accomplish our "to do" lists, so we end up clocking long hours. This works for the short haul, but over time it becomes burdensome, leading to burnout and adversely affecting productivity.

The answers to these questions can provide a foundation for understanding the value of work in people terms. Once you know who does what and how, now comes the hard part: What is the role of the manager? To my way of thinking, managers have two prime responsibilities: Provide resources and remove obstacles. Each of these responsibilities can provide insights into the what, who, and how of workflow.

Purpose very often works best when tied to the strategic plan. The first time that Consumers Union (under the tenure of CEO Jim Guest) rolled out a strategic plan, employees did not understand how their work fit into the plan. So, when the organization developed a new plan, it communicated it throughout the company by holding meetings and workshops. Now, as Guest reports, when people debate ideas, they ask: "How does this fit with the five goals of our strategic plan?"[11] Such clarity may seem simple, but it does link purpose to results and, more important, connects people's jobs to the plan.

When speaking of purpose, Guest likes to relate the story that Peter Drucker told about the stonemason. A visitor to town encounters a stonemason and asks him what he is doing. The man replies that he is cutting stone. Another mason replies that he is building a wall. But a third mason replies with pride, "I am building a cathedral." Taking pride into what you do comes when you know the purpose, the big picture, how your work contributes to the whole—the cathedral you are building.

Providing resources is a matter of assigning the right people to the right task at the right time. The manager's challenge comes in looking beneath this mantra to determine if the people are truly right for the job—that is, do they have the right skills and training to do the work? Next, you need to figure out if they have the resources at hand to do the job in the given time frame. In theory, sure they do; in practice, not so often. That is where good managers improvise; they find ways to get quality work done with fewer resources. It requires good planning and also insight into the people doing the work. Allocating resources is one thing; finding the right people to manage those resources and use them efficiently may be more important.

Therefore, you need to know what your people are capable of doing. Such knowledge comes from observing them in the workplace. You turn loose those who can do the job. For those who are not yet ready, you provide training. But sometimes it becomes obvious that certain employees are not up to the task. That leads into a manager's second responsibility: removing obstacles.

First, a manager needs to identify the problem. When an employee is not capable of doing what is asked, the manager needs to act. For example, an engineer may be asked to move into a sales role. Some people may enjoy the challenge, but for others it may be an unwelcome stretch of talent and skill. Engineers are problem solvers, and as introverts, they typically like to pursue solutions by themselves. Sales people are good at identifying problems, but since the nature of their role calls for them to serve their customers, they need to find others to fix things for them. As extroverts, this role suits them. Mixing the roles can be tricky, so when an engineer is unhappy or unproductive in a sales role, the manager must move the engineer back to engineering and fill the sales slot with a capable sales person.

It is one thing to react to problems; it is another thing to go looking for them. The principles of *kaizen*, or seeking continuous improvement, necessarily challenge managers to look for bottlenecks or holdups to productivity. Sometimes the roadblock is a lack of resources or inadequate ones. Other times the obstacle is the management system itself. Reporting systems by nature often hamstring operations because they require employees to get approval for every step they take. This is a form of validation, but it can be time consuming as well as onerous. Reducing, not eliminating, such reporting can speed up the flow.

Likewise, managers themselves can be roadblocks. A manager who needs to sign off on every decision is not only slowing things down, he or she may also be preventing direct reports from figuring things out for themselves. Or, let us say a team is working to plan and meet deadlines. That is good, but what if the team is capable of doing more? It would behoove the manager to find how much more they can do and then decide if it's worth pursuing. In either case, the manager needs to make a decision that will enable the team to optimize its workflow by letting employees manage the process and solve their own problems when possible.

Taking time to determine the what, how, and who of work, coupled with an attention to providing resources and removing obstacles, lays the foundation for the leader to begin to figure out how to help the people on his or her team achieve their best.

Driving High Performance

Purpose is an intention, but if it is to succeed it must be used to drive results. One way leaders can utilize purpose as an engine for helping the organization achieve its intentions is to link purpose to execution. That is, you link what the organization does (its *mission*) to how it does it (its *values and behaviors*).

• **Know the mission.** Mission is the anchor. It is the foundation upon which the organization rises. Put simply, mission defines what the company does, whether it builds houses, provides medical care, or produces entertainment. Mission is the "what" of the enterprise. It may be the most obvious fact of any organization, but all too often managers fail to communicate the mission to their employees. When that occurs, vagueness replaces clarity. And when that happens, employees are left to wonder how what they do matters. By contrast, when the mission is clear, people know it and have the opportunity to embrace it.

• **Understand the values.** If mission is the "what," then values establish the "how." Values are what hold the organization together. You can consider values as the set of principles that underscore purpose—that is, what we believe and why we believe it. In the military, the values are duty, service, and honor. Soldiers know these values and how they shape the culture in which they serve. Values in the private sector may be less defined, but they are nonetheless important to how an organization functions. When values are clearly defined, employees can use them as guides to shape behavior, specifically in terms of how people treat one another.

• **Know the roles and responsibilities.** When employees understand their role as it pertains to the mission, they can do their jobs with a greater sense of purpose. That is, when an accountant understands that how he manages accounts payable affects the bottom line, he knows how his actions impact corporate performance. Likewise, when a human resources manager is clear on mission, she can develop and manage programs that enable employees to deliver on it more effectively. Responsibilities, too, need to be defined so that employees understand what part of the mission they will be accountable for.

• **Create opportunities.** Mission and values are fundamental, but in themselves they lack momentum. Movement comes from translating purpose into action. But before that can happen, you need to think about what needs doing and why. The act of creation for an organization becomes that of translating purpose into roles and responsibilities—that is, into who does what. Creating also includes thinking about possibilities. Even when the mission is clear, there may be many ways to fulfill it. Leaders must determine the best path forward and that is why creativity matters.

• **Encourage collaboration.** Clarity in purpose as it relates to mission, values, and creativity enables employees to share an understanding of what is expected of them. They have what is necessary to work together, but even better, they have the impetus to collaborate.

Shared knowledge and values enable collaboration, but they cannot ensure it. Genuine collaboration will come only when people want to do it and can trust one another. A component of collaboration may be shared sacrifice—that is, giving up one choice to make a better choice that will enable a better result. True collaboration comes when ideas and actions are combined to achieve something that individuals working separately could not achieve.

• **Achieve execution.** Getting the job done is the prerequisite for success. Purpose sets up what needs to be done, but employees determine what actually gets done. They must be capable and competent, as well as have the tools and resources necessary to complete the job. Performance depends on capable execution by employees who are engaged in what they do. Their commitment to the task depends on their ability to attend to the task at hand in such a way that the organization fulfills its purpose.

Improving Performance

Purpose can be a powerful catalyst to performance when it is channeled in ways that enable employees to see what is expected of the organization and what is expected of them to help the organization achieve its intended results.

Pat Williams, Senior Vice President of the Orlando Magic and motivational speaker, says that putting people first comes down to liking people. He quotes Eddie Robinson, the legendary football coach at Grambling University, as saying, "You can't coach 'em if you don't love 'em." This was a philosophy that basketball coach John Wooden embraced. As Williams, who wrote *Coach Wooden: The 7 Principles*

That Shaped His Life and Will Change Yours, recalls, Wooden would say, "I'm not going to like all of you equally, but I am going to try to love all of you equally." Contrast this attitude with that of former U.S. president Richard Nixon, who was not comfortable around and did not like most people. As Williams puts it, "A lot of us are self-centered, but if we don't have a heart and love for people, then it's awfully hard to be a world-class leader."[12]

Players will compete hard for a coach they know cares about them as people. Expressing that sense of caring is essential. Williams explains, "You don't have to be buddy-buddy, but just show an interest in them, their families, and even their outside interests. Learn what makes them tick. That may be the heart and soul of leadership."[13]

"You're only as strong as your people make you," says Roger Webb, President of the University of Central Oklahoma. "You have to let them identify with you." It is important for leaders to demonstrate that the contribution employees make is important "to the overall success of the operation." Webb takes that identification process personally. Watching him walk through campus is an exercise in patience. Everywhere he goes people want to chat with him, and Webb makes time for everyone: faculty, staff, and students. For years, Webb has taught a class in leadership to freshmen, a practice he not only enjoys but one that he feels keeps him close to what students are thinking and doing.

"You have to find ways to let [people] know you're concerned about them," says Webb. "So, you ask questions about their families and how they are doing. Little things matter in establishing rapport with your colleagues and your people." Webb has found a way to institutionalize such concern. For example, in Oklahoma, severe weather is a concern in the late spring, so when bad weather is imminent, school closes to allow employees to pick up their children.[14]

You can demonstrate concern for employees by rewarding them financially, too. In 2010, the university had accumulated healthy cash reserves owing to increased enrollments, so Webb decided to take a million dollars of the reserve and award bonuses to every faculty member, including part-time faculty. It was a small gesture, but it was recognition of the faculty's contribution to growing student enrollment.[15]

One man who illustrates what Marshall Goldsmith means by finding your own purpose was a roofer in Goldsmith's hometown of Valley Station, Kentucky. As a teenager, Goldsmith helped the man, Dennis Mudd, install a roof on the family home. When the job was done, he said to Goldsmith's father, "Bill, please inspect the roof. If it's of high quality, pay me. If it's not of high quality, it's all free." Goldsmith notes that Mudd was poor, but there was something in that statement that inspired him to think, "I want to be him when I grow up."[16]

Mudd found purpose in his work and led Goldsmith to develop his own results-based model of executive coaching: If you see results, pay; if not, there is no charge. Mudd also drove a school bus and spent a few minutes every day talking to the school kids about life. Goldsmith marvels that Mudd "managed to instill purpose in both his jobs." Goldsmith sums it up with, "I think the best leaders can do to instill purpose is to challenge others to find purpose within themselves rather than telling them what their purpose is."[17]

Accountability Is Essential

Followership is rooted in purpose. John Maxwell, the bestselling leadership author and entrepreneur, believes it comes down to three qualities in a leader: caring, assistance, and character. People will follow a leader who shows his heart, is there to help others, and is trustworthy.

For Maxwell, followership is essential to accountability. "Never put out the vision; that is, never draw the picture without putting yourself in it," he says. "I'm not going to ask my people to do something I won't do. I'm not going to ask my people to sacrifice something I won't sacrifice. I'm not going to ask them to go somewhere I won't go." When others sense a leader's personal commitment, according to Maxwell, they are more willing "to step up to the plate" and be accountable along with him or her.[18]

When it comes to accountability, Marshall Goldsmith, who has coached more than 300 CEOs in his decades-long career says, "Leaders should be the role models for living the values of the corporation. They should get ongoing feedback about how their behavior is aligned with the corporate values." Toward that end, he adds, "leaders need to stand up publicly and talk about what they are doing to improve their own performance in terms of living the values." It is not enough for them to "preach at employees."[19]

Goldsmith believes that "every company has the same values, basically." To illustrate this point, he relates a story about watching a CEO deliver a powerfully moving speech about ethics, integrity, and values. To accompany the CEO's presentation was an inspirational video costing some half a million dollars to produce. "The name of the company was Enron." Coincidentally, according to a bestselling book on Enron, *Conspiracy of Fools* by then–*New York Times* reporter Kurt Eichenwald, it was at that corporate off-site where Enron's first illegal scheme was hatched. "What I learned," says Goldsmith, "is that our values are not what we say; our values are what we do."[20]

When it comes to accountability, Tammy Erickson, award-winning author and consultant, believes that leaders owe it to their followers to be honest. "We would want our friends to be honest with us, to tell us when things change. We'd want our spouses to. We would like our corporate leaders to hold those same standards in the workplace." As Erickson, who specializes in generational work issues, explains, "It's not so much what you do, it's the way in which you do it."[21]

To instill a culture of accountability, University of San Diego professor George Reed suggests that the leader "needs to cultivate people that speak truth to power, cultivating people around you who will give it to you straight, frank, and honest." The concept of "managing by walking around" is valid; it allows people to see, hear, and connect with you. Reed also advises holding "skip level" meetings, where an executive meets with those one or two levels down. The intent is not to supervise a direct report, but to facilitate direct interaction with upper management. If done regularly, employees can get used to speaking their minds to those who run the organization.[22]

Direct contact with employees at all levels is important. Not only does it demonstrate a leader's involvement with people, it is also a way to get unfiltered information. "The reason people are modifying information is not because they want to be deceitful," says Reed. "It's because they desperately want to please the boss." At every level on the organizational ladder there is an opportunity for distortion, according to Reed. "What I tell executives is if you're in meetings and the PowerPoints are perfect . . . you're probably being overly filtered." To fight that process, Reed says, "get out more or find some trusted advisers who can go down there and find out what the ground truth really looks like."[23]

Avoiding message massaging and information distortion is a premise behind the hit reality television show *Undercover Boss.* Each episode features a CEO working on the lowest rung of his or her organization's ladder. It mimics the premise of Mark Twain's novel *The Prince and the Pauper*, in which a royal disguises himself to experience the life of a commoner. CEOs certainly need not go to extremes to get information, but they need to find ways to meet and mingle with employees as a means of discovering how things in their company really work. Otherwise, they are flying blind.

Vineet Nayar, CEO of HCL Technologies, a global IT services firm headquartered in India, cautions executives about what he calls "assumed leadership." He explains, "Just because you are sitting in the corner office you assume that people respect you, and because you work fourteen hours a day seven days a week, you assume people trust you." Executives also assume falsely that since their immediate staff understands the corporate strategy, everyone else in the company does, too.[24]

To ward against such thinking, Nayar offers three prescriptions. One, be accountable for your communications. It is a leader's responsibility. Two, stop thinking that you need to have all of the answers. "This puts [the leader] on a pedestal where he can only fail." Three, follow through on your commitments. "People believe what you expect them to do, you should do yourself." That is, leaders need to hold themselves accountable for behaviors they expect of others as well as for positions they advocate. In other words, if a leader expects his management team to act in a transparent fashion, he had better practice the same. Likewise, if a leader advocates for social responsibility or sustainability, he must follow through on such commitments.[25]

Good leaders that Nayar has known do not "come to a job for a purpose. They have a purpose" already. Since such leaders are comfortable with themselves, they can "instill a sense of purpose in the workplace because that is the only way they know how to work." In addition, Nayar says, "Employees are the center of your future. . . . I am in the business of enthusing, encouraging, enabling employees. . . . I am not the one who's creating value [for customers]. I hold myself accountable to my employees who are in the value zone." According to Nayar, employees create the value and "drive" corporate growth. As a result, executives and employees are accountable to each other.[26]

Accountability reinforces purpose. It is the foundation upon which leaders can build a high-performance organization that depends on people at every level working together to achieve the mission. Knowing that the mission stands for something purposeful gives greater impetus to achieving meaningful results.

Instill Purpose in People: Survey Results

What Employees and Managers Say

More than 80 percent of those surveyed say that leaders can best demonstrate that they truly do put people first by:

- Delivering intrinsic awards (comp time, bonuses, etc.)
- Offering developmental opportunities
- Providing timely recognition
- Promoting from within

Three-quarters of respondents believe providing competitive compensation is a strong indication that leaders put people first.

What Leaders Must Do

"Putting people first" is a platitude unless it is put into action. Recognition and rewards are essential, especially when done in a timely fashion. Over and above this, employees want the opportunity to grow their careers; that is why promoting from within resonates. Leaders reinforce the possibility of promotion when they give employees the opportunity to develop their talents and learn new skills. Compensation is important, of course; employees want to feel as if their labor is valued.

How to Inspire Purposeful People

Leadership Questions

- What do I do to honor the spirit that my employees bring to work every day?

- How well do I show my appreciation to my team?

Leadership Directives

- Communicate the organization's vision to all employees. Be clear, coherent, and consistent.

- Ask teams to develop vision statements that complement the organizational vision.

- Find ways to make the mission tangible to all employees—that is, link it to job function and job task. Make the connection between what an employee does and how that job complements purpose.

- Set clear expectations for behaviors that model organizational values. Hold yourself accountable first.

- Find ways to reward individual achievements.

- Create a culture of recognition that is timely and meaningful. Pats on the back are great, but find ways to show employees that you and the organization truly care about them as contributors.

CHAPTER 3

MAKE AMBIGUITY COMFORTABLE BY CLARIFYING PURPOSE

> "The first essential for advancement in knowledge is for men
> to be willing to say, 'We do not know.'"
>
> **—ROGER BACON, THIRTEENTH CENTURY ENGLISH PHILOSOPHER**

"Every day you read what a terrible age we live in. Well, I've heard that all my life," said Horton Foote to Terry Gross, host of NPR's *Fresh Air* radio program in 1988. "I don't think any age is any worse. There are just new [and different] problems is all."[1] Foote knew of what he spoke. A native Texan, Horton Foote, who died in 2009 at the age of 92, was one of America's greatest playwrights, although for most of his life he labored in a kind of obscurity, despite having won two Academy Awards, one for the screen adaptation of Harper Lee's book *To Kill a Mockingbird* and the second for the original screenplay for the film *Tender Mercies*.

Foote's plays, and he wrote some 40, were about the simple things experienced by the people he grew up with in small-town Texas. So often the stories involved loss and adversity, people struggling against the odds to make sense of life's hardships. There was joy, too, as strength of character and love frequently prevailed. So Foote's comment about terrible times is rooted in circumstances in which people felt a loss of control and that the odds may have been against them. Yet, so often, as Foote expressed in his writings, they prevailed.

Hard times provoke a certain unease that accompanies not knowing what comes next. As with the Great Depression, people remain uneasy, even when better times are clearly in view. We think, "What if this happens again? What if the bad times return? How will we make it?" These questions present leaders with opportunity. Taking the long view of history is one way to make sense of the madness of today.

●　　●　　●　　●　　●　　●　　●

As uncertain as things may seem today, modern crises pale against the backdrop of American history. The outcome of the American Revolution was never certain until the very end, six years after shots were first fired, and even then, the establishment of the new nation took another seven years. Then, the integrity of the Union was torn asunder in the Civil War, and it took four long years of fighting, the bloodiest in our history, to bring it back together. Another century would pass before "equal justice before the law" would apply to all citizens. In hindsight, perhaps owing to too many John Wayne–type movies, the Second World War seems more a pageant than a painful struggle that required the mobilization of 12 million civilians. That war's end offered peace, but it deteriorated into the Cold War, which brought the United States and the USSR into conflicts both hot (Korea and Vietnam) and frightful (the Berlin Airlift and the Cuban Missile Crisis).

Our nation has experienced a number of economic depressions, only the last of which (1929–late 1930s) we call the Great Depression. Recessions are too many to count—at least seven since the mid-seventies. Each of these recessions brought people into confrontation with things greater than themselves and too often put them in seemingly unwinnable situations.

The good news is that we have always prevailed. The nation and its people have held together. But today's challenges are not regional; they are global. And although global trade has been a boon to the developing as well as the developed world, for many less-educated workers in the United States and Europe, cheaper labor in Asia and South Asia has brought high rates of unemployment. The recent Great Recession eradicated more than eight million jobs and created staggering levels of uncertainty.

Ambiguity Is a Constant

"The ambiguity of the present is matched by the ambiguity of the past," says Dan Denison of IMD business school. In other words, we have always faced challenges. They may seem greater today because they occur with greater speed and they are uncertain to us now. According to Denison, "There is always a premium on being able to deal with the unknown. People will venture there if they feel they'll be secure in doing it. It is a leader's job to create that sense of security." On the other hand, "Fear, uncertainty, and doubt are things that will kill innovation."[2]

A leader must make people feel comfortable taking risks. Call it "expeditionary marketing," a term coined by the late management thinker, professor, and author C. K. Prahalad.[3] According to Denison, this means that "you try something new, you stick out your neck so that you could learn from the experience."[4]

"The only way you can make people comfortable with the unknown is to be comfortable with it yourself," says leadership author John Maxwell. "People really sense when a leader is uncomfortable or uncertain about what is in the future. Leaders have to be comfortable with something before they can make [others] comfortable with it."[5]

Maxwell knows the feeling firsthand. He was a pastor for 25 years. His church had decided to relocate—something that would cost $40 million. Leaders of the church were understandably nervous, but Maxwell took the time to express his confidence in the project and how comfortable he was with the decision. After a short time, Maxwell could tell that his audience was feeling more relaxed about the decision. Maxwell had to do the same with his congregation. As he says, "Nothing makes followers more nervous . . . more uncertain, than to have a leader that is uncertain. But once they see confidence and assurance, there is a transference of feelings." They grow more comfortable. "You cannot omit words," says Maxwell, but those words must reflect the leader's sense of honesty.[6]

When it comes to dealing with ambiguity, retired Marine brigadier general Tom Draude talks about "the four Fs of combat leadership: fatigue, fear, failure, and feelings." When he was serving as Assistant Division Commander in Operation Desert Storm, he made a point of speaking to commissioned and noncommissioned officers about what they might expect once battle commenced. He was specific about the need to "use cohesion in a unit . . . to counteract fear," as well as a buffer against the feelings leaders experience when they suffer casualties.[7]

Draude notes that leaders are "often anxious to get into the how of change without explaining the why." He would tell his Marines (and later, his employees), "Now, I want those of you who are closer to the problem than we are to help me with this. . . . If you can explain the why [of the unknown] most people can live with it."[8]

A lament that Michael Useem, professor at the University of Pennsylvania's Wharton School of Business, often hears is, "I'm trying to get my job done. If only the guys at the top would tell me where we're going, I can do it." Employees are crying out for clarity. Useem maintains that "leaders need to be more aggressive [about] telling the strategy story—where we are going and how we're going to get there." They must frame that story so that "people on the front lines can hear and digest it. A memo won't do. An annual report is insufficient." It takes active participation." According to Useem, "the best leaders I've encountered are those who will themselves and their staffs to speak to as many employees as possible in a 12-month cycle." You can do it in small group meetings or large off-sites. The challenge is to "manage by walking around," as the leader does, explains Useem, "articulating the vision, the mission, and the strategy again and again."[9] And, as Useem adds, the rationale must be included in that articulation. It is not enough to state a goal; you need to tell people why the strategy matters and why what they do matters in fulfilling that strategy.

Leaders Show the Way

For Vineet Nayar, people are essential to a growth strategy. The CEO of HCL Technologies, Nayar believes "you have to create what I call an 'organization of innovation.'" Purpose stems from allowing people to create at the grassroots level. Toward that end, says Nayar, "you need to put people at the center for your strategy to be able to attract the best, retain the best, motivate the best, and get the best out of the best."[10]

When it comes to dealing with uncertainty, Nayar adopts a non-Western perspective: "The biggest ambiguity when a child is born is what the child will do in life. You cannot be more ambiguous than that." In many parts of Asia, there is a custom of the grandmother picking up the infant and pronouncing what the child will become, be it a scientist, an artist, or a businessperson. Family members remind the child of what the grandmother said about him or her at birth, and that may help the child choose a direction in life.

Ambiguity is necessary, argues Nayar, carrying over his analogy to the business world. "If it does not exist, it must be created because the future . . . is uncertain." Next, a leader must "convert ambiguity into positivity." Leaders should look at ambiguity as opportunity, rather than as something negative. Nayar concludes, "If you create a culture [in which] people like ambiguity, there are no rights and wrongs" when it comes to experimentation. Such a culture inspires people to be creative.[11]

Nayar draws a distinction between ambiguity and probability. For example, Google is relentlessly innovative when it creates multiple products, hoping that one or two may succeed. "That's probability," says Nayar. Contrast that with the motion picture company that produces one picture at a time: That's ambiguity because the company doesn't know if the picture will become a hit. Its leaders must "create excitement around that ambiguity," so that people feel comfortable with it.

There are times of uncertainty, however, when you have to "go with the flow," or as Nayar puts it, "allow yourself to drift," as on a river. By not resisting the current, you conserve energy that you can use when issues become clearer and the course ahead seems more certain.[12]

Nayar likes to tell the story of his days studying mechanical engineering. One day the professor came into the classroom, in which an engine was mounted, and he said, "Open it up." The students eagerly tore apart the engine in short order. Then the professor said, "Okay, put it back together." He then walked out of the classroom, leaving the students to piece it together by themselves. It took them a month, but they accomplished the task. "What the class taught me," recalls Nayar, "is that if you are not allowed to make mistakes, if you are not given space to make mistakes, how can you create miracles?" In business, this means creating successful innovations—things that turn into products and services that customers desire.[13]

Leading with Eyes Wide Open

Much of innovation occurs by making mistakes, by not knowing what will come next. "Business decisions are based on intuition," says Nayar. "You go in with an assumption, but you keep your eyes and ears open [so that] you can change the course of your decision [if] what you see in front of you is different from what you assumed."[14] Leaders need to "trust their gut," of course; but when what they have assumed turns out differently, they need to be flexible enough to change direction. That, too, is part of a culture of innovation because it allows for creativity at the same time as it opens the door for doing things differently if circumstances dictate. Consider it as a disciplined form of innovation.

Michael Useem of the Wharton School credits Nayar with "painting a picture with the office of the CEO at the bottom of the pyramid, not at the top." There is symbolism in Nayar's actions, says Useem, but Nayar and colleagues like him are "following up with actions that make consistent sense," ones that employees understand and appreciate. That is important because "it all begins in the corner office." According to Useem, "Leadership is more vital in a period of uncertainty and change than when life is not changing, when markets are predictable. When there is greater uncertainty, greater ambiguity, it's at that very moment that leadership is more critical."[15]

But leadership is not a solo act. As Useem explains, "it's also more incumbent upon the leader to draw upon the known and instincts of people in the ranks." Therefore, as he sees it, "getting people more comfortable with uncertainty and ambiguity is also a matter of reminding them that their ideas, their read of the moment, their thinking ought to be presented to people in leadership positions." In such times, leaders need the right input at the right time. "Ambiguity requires the complete engagement of everyone in the ranks."[16]

"What we need now are leaders who can recognize what they don't know, who acknowledge that they don't have to be the smartest people in the room," says George Reed, the retired Army officer who teaches at the University of San Diego. Leaders, he feels, must be able "to say 'I understand you need direction so I'm going to give it to you, but we may have to go in a different direction tomorrow.' And that's because the environment's changing so fast."[17]

One general for whom Reed worked in the Army did exactly that. He would say, "Folks, I'm not exactly sure what the right answer is on this thing. But I know you need direction so I want you to go this way. Hold on to that loosely because tomorrow I may come back and tell you to go another way because we're continuing to collect information." He also invited people who disagreed with him to voice their opinions.

Reed asserts that this approach works conceptually, but can be hard tactically, when progress is based on executing directives. Too much change precludes accomplishment, because people are always having to throw out what they just did and begin anew. That can be frustrating. "I think that one of the important roles that leaders can take is to give people things to hang on to," says Reed. "It may not be a strategic direction because that's changing based upon the environment, but it could relate to values, which are not going to change." Reed suggests that a leader could say, "I am not sure about what the future will bring but here's what you can count on. I care about you and you care about me. If we have that, we can weather everything else."[18]

Understanding Uncertainty as a Norm

Michelle Rhee, former chancellor of the Washington, D.C., public schools, likes to hire people who are comfortable with ambiguity. As she recalls saying to teacher candidates, "If you are somebody who needs to be out of the office every day at six o'clock . . . this is probably not the place for you." This job, Rhee would explain, requires working in an "incredibly dynamic and ever-changing environment. We need people who can stop on a dime, turn, and head in the other direction if that's what makes sense."[19]

Rhee believes in "flattening the organization." Bureaucracy, such as she found in the D.C. district, "stifles good conversation, innovation, and creativity." To get around it, Rhee made a regular effort to speak directly to parents, teachers, principals, and even interns. She recognized that suggestions for improvement can come from anywhere. "You want to give people the freedom and flexibility to make mistakes," she explained. But there must be a balance with good practice. "We are dealing with children and we cannot be reckless about it."[20]

Accountability is personal to Michelle Rhee. When the man who hired her, Adrian Fenty, did not win reelection as mayor, Rhee stepped down, too. Prior to her leaving, Rhee said, "I should absolutely be held accountable at the highest level."

"Different generations tend to approach ambiguity differently," says Tammy Erickson, who has conducted extensive research into generational issues in the workplace. She describes Gen Xers—workers born in the Sixties and Seventies—as more comfortable with it because their formative years were spent in times of economic uncertainty. "It's not something they even question. It's just part of who they are," she explains. Older workers, on the other hand, are more comfortable with certainty; anything that disrupts their goals is unsettling.[21]

When speaking of trust, Erickson is a realist: "You don't trust in the abstract. You trust in something." She suggests that if people feel they have been given short shrift by those in authority, it is harder for them to trust their leadership: "People aren't trusting the old loyalty equations that have existed between employers and employees." As Erickson points out, employees do not expect to have a job for life; yet employers have not "defined a new equation" for loyalty. As a result, employees "mourn" its passing without moving forward.[22]

"It starts with hiring people who are wired to be comfortable with the unknown," says Tom Monahan, Chairman and CEO of the Corporate Executive Board, a consulting firm that "supplies information, data, and best practices" to companies around the world. "Expertise is sometimes the enemy of comfort with ambiguity, because expertise is the ability to master a known situation.'" Monahan looks for people who he says are "serial masters, [who] have found different ways to master different situations."[23]

One technique that Monahan has found for dealing with the vagaries produced in uncertain situations is storytelling. Although ambiguity is often perceived as a negative, Monahan believes that it need not be so. "Serendipity is a form of ambiguity," says Monahan. "You have to go out of your way to communicate it." For example, when things go unexpectedly right, "you got lucky. When things change, it's not always a deterioration. It's a reminder that deviation from the mean can happen in both directions." Organizations, asserts Monahan, "get flustered" when things go wrong. That is why stories about what went right, when the team exceeded their goals, are important. They provide a kind of compass for navigating the unexpected.[24]

Monahan emphasizes that it is necessary to be straight with people. Too often when a team does what is expected, management says it did a great job. Conversely, if the team fails, management might castigate the group. He says that it is important to be honest about the situations and the assumptions made about them. Success may be the result of good fortune; at the same time, in cases of failure, it might be possible to say, "The team did a heroic job with some of our core assumptions about what was going to happen. They didn't hold up to be true." Critical analysis helps people come to grips with ambiguity, because they can decide whether failure was a people problem or the result of faulty assumptions. "Pulling apart the intrinsic assumptions from the efforts and creativity of the people executing the plan is important to making people feel comfortable with ambiguity," Monahan concludes.[25]

Vineet Nayar, of HCL Technologies, relates a story of tribal people in India who happened to live on top of a huge deposit of bauxite. Naturally, mining companies wanted to extract the bauxite, but the tribals, who do not partake of the modern world in terms of education, medicine, or even sanitation, wanted nothing more than to be left alone. "The hill is their god," explains Nayar. It is the place where their ancestors have lived for generations, and they do not want to move.

Such an example is not wholly uncommon in India, which, Nayar says, lives simultaneously in three different centuries: the sixteenth, the twentieth, and the twenty-first. Some 300 million people live in each of these centuries. A leader cannot focus on what separates people but, rather, on what unites them. A leader must look for a convergence of values and opportunities so that people with different mindsets can benefit. "The art of management involves a lot of patience, empathy, and understanding," says Nayar. "Alternate points of view are okay." A leader must "focus on making progress rather than changing the world."[26]

"I think the leader has to be comfortable with ambiguity," says Jim Guest, President and CEO of Consumers Union. "I thrive on ambiguity." That is good for Consumers Union as a publisher of information (*Consumer Reports*) that consumers use to make informed purchasing decisions. Like all publishers, it has migrated many of its services from traditional print to the web. It was a change that was uncomfortable for some employees, but over time they became accustomed to it, recognized that it was necessary, and ultimately embraced it. Going through the change together and experiencing success helped people become more comfortable with the change process.

Not everything went smoothly, however. Guest tells a story about offering a car's glove-compartment organizer as a premium for new subscribers. The organizer contained, among other things, a tire pressure gauge and flashlight. The premium stimulated new subscriptions, but the gauge didn't work and the flashlight overheated. Two of the marketing people came to Guest to apologize. He assured them that they had done what he had challenged them to do: Be creative and entrepreneurial. And so Guest suggested, "Let's do the best recall anybody has ever done; we're big on safety." Consumers Union reported the problem to the Consumer Product Safety Commission and gave new subscribers a "free subscription for a year if they disposed of the flawed products."

Guest was also insistent that such problems not keep staff from thinking outside the box. "Don't let this [problem] make you gun-shy about taking risks in the future," he told them. Guest sent an e-mail to the staff "praising the marketing team as a way of reinforcing the concept that it was okay to take risks. It's okay to make mistakes." Or, as Guest puts it, "so rather than heads rolling, people got a pat on the back."[27]

Taking Responsibility for Uncertainty

As part of the setup for each question posed to employees, a leader can open with, "Here's how I see it." Then follow up with, "What do you think?" This question-and-answer process presents a dialogue between boss and direct report that gives each the opportunity to express his or her views.

Marshall Goldsmith believes strongly in the concept of "mutual responsibility" when it comes to times of rapid change. "While managers can be effective in letting people know their views, their vision, their direction, and their feedback, employees need to be given the responsibility of talking to the manager if there is doubt or ambiguity about goals and objectives." In periods of transition, these things will change, but Goldsmith believes "there's no excuse for any employee to have confusion about what their priorities or directions are." As obvious as it may seem to assure employees that they can speak up, Goldsmith maintains that "most people underestimate the degree of difficulty in communication, especially during periods of rapid change and ambiguity." Providing structure for conversations to occur can give both manager and employee the framework they need to connect one-on-one.[28]

With regard to ambiguity, Roger Webb, president of UCO, says, "You have to recognize the uncertainty of the times in which we live and [the fact that] dealing with perpetual change" is a reality. People have a choice, emphasizes Webb, to treat change as an ally or as a fear. A leader's job is to anticipate changes, but with technological change, it is hard to prepare. At the same time, a leader needs to reassure people that the organization will survive the changes it is facing.[29]

"You can never be totally comfortable with ambiguity. That's why it's called ambiguity," says Marshall Goldsmith. He suggests six questions that leaders can regularly ask their people:[30]

1. Where do you think we should be going?
2. Where do you think you and your part of the business should be going?
3. What do you think you're doing well?
4. If you were the leader, what ideas would you have for you?
5. How can I help?
6. What suggestions or ideas do you have for me?

Goldsmith believes that making a habit of asking these questions will help people feel more comfortable with the notion of ambiguity. The answers they evoke should lead people to understand more clearly what is expected of them and what they can do themselves to prepare for what may happen next.

Methods for Dealing with Ambiguity

Dealing with a crisis big or small tests the mettle of any executive. It is particularly tough now because few, if any, have dealt with an economic crisis as severe as the one we face today. Suddenly, a topic that is not taught in business schools has appeared out of nowhere, standing front and center. It's called ambiguity. Fortunately there are methods for dealing with it:

- **Square the circle.** Look at your situation in terms of what you know. Itemize the known quantities—that is, what you can control, whether that is cost, quality, resources, or other factors. Draw a boundary around that list. Outside this boundary lie factors such as competition, consumer spending, government policy, and global trends—that is, factors you cannot control. Then, leverage your strengths; use them to give you clarity about your operations so that you are prepared to deal with any crises that emerge from "outside the circle." For example, get your cost structure in line, but also spend time developing your people through methods such as cross-training and job rotation.

- **Be pragmatic.** The American philosopher of pragmatism, William James, wrote, "The greatest discovery of my generation is that a human being can alter his life by altering his attitudes"; on which Franklin Roosevelt, an ardent admirer of James, expounded, "The only limit to our realization of tomorrow will be our doubts of today."[31] The lodestar of American capitalism has been entrepreneurism. Even today, most new jobs come from small businesses, many of them new businesses. In addition, established businesses seek to be innovative to adapt to changing conditions. New and old businesses that succeed are the ones that do things—they experiment.

- **Keep trying, even in light of failure.** More than 90 percent of all new products fail. That's reality. The challenge is to keep moving forward and realize that failure is part of the management process. As they say in NASCAR, "if you ain't rubbin,' you ain't racin.'" That means you need to nudge, push, and jostle your way to the finish line. To do so, you must stimulate your people to try new and different ways of doing things. Innovation is not limited to new offerings. Challenge people to develop new and better ways of operating as a business; processes top to bottom can be examined for ways to take out waste and repetition, in favor of returning meaning to function and value to customers.

- **Remain resolute.** Failure is never desired, but it can be an outcome. You need to weigh the cost of failure against the cost of doing nothing. Standing still in our boggy economy likely means you will sink to your knees unless you pick up one foot after another and keep moving forward. Recall FDR's words as he sought to use government as an instrument of recovery during the first term of his presidency: "If it fails, admit it frankly and try another. But above all, try something."[32]

- **Spread cheer.** The economic situation we are going through is unprecedented for recent times. The worst may or may not be over in terms of unemployment levels, so it is up to the leaders on the ground to maintain perspective. They must lead from the front, dispensing confidence and good cheer. This is not being Pollyannaish; it is what leaders have always done in a crisis. We follow leaders not because they bring us down but because they lift our spirits with their attitude, words, and examples.

Management is a discipline that establishes the metrics by which businesses can gauge performance in everything from quality, cost, and speed to productivity, including human capital. Ambiguity is, therefore, the antithesis of this discipline, and that is why so many managers are uncomfortable with uncertainty. Some may never adjust, but those who do, especially those who are beginning their careers or hitting their stride, may just need to become more comfortable with it.

Since the "new normal" for today's business world has yet to be established, leaders must adapt their style. To effectively lead others through the morass, it is not enough to have a compass. Metaphorically speaking, you will also need a boat, a car, and a plane to get through, around, or over the obstacles that are in your way.

"Leaders have the finished product in their minds," says Pat Williams, a bestselling author and in-demand speaker. "They see the victory already taking place. Then they work backwards, inspiring people, giving them confidence." That, according to Williams, was critical to Franklin D. Roosevelt's ability to bring people together in the Great Depression. He radiated confidence through his words, his looks, and his vision.[33]

Leaders need to become comfortable with the unknown; over time, the unknown may become as familiar as the established norms of the past. Ambiguity may never be as easy to understand, but it will become navigable. We in business had grown accustomed to growth as a universal right. It is a right no longer. In business, black and white is a luxury; gray is the new norm. Having a strong sense of purpose and projecting that purpose onto your employees will lead them to think and act in ways that help the organization thrive.

Make Ambiguity Acceptable: Survey Results

What Employees and Managers Say

More than 85 percent of those surveyed believe that leaders can effect the biggest difference in making people comfortable with the unknown by:

- Providing vision
- Setting clear expectations
- Engaging in planning

Over 80 percent of respondents believe that leaders provide a feeling of certainty when they allow employees to dialogue with key stakeholders, and nearly two-thirds say that studying business trends is advantageous to dealing with uncertainty.

What Leaders Must Do

The pace of change has speeded up in our lifetime; in fact, the status quo no longer exists. Watching trends is critical, for it provides the perspective on new factors that can influence the present and future of the organization. Also, leaders need to find ways to assure employees that change is not something to fear but, rather, something to embrace. That's easy to say, but rarely done. When a leader backs that concept with a vision supported by clear expectations, he or she provides an avenue for employees to see the positive possibilities of change and assess what is in it for them. Leaders who urge employees to meet with customers, vendors, and shareholders give those employees an opportunity to learn for themselves.

How to Provide Clarity for the Organization

Leadership Questions

- How well does my team understand what is expected of them?

- How well have I made it known that my role is to support the mission of the team?

Leadership Directives

- Make it known that there is no such thing as a dumb question. Ignorance thrives when people do not ask questions.

- Teach critical thinking skills: how to assess a situation, consider the variables, and make an informed decision.

- Challenge managers to make decisions based on what they know now, rather than waiting for all the variables to be determined.

- Encourage seasoned managers to make decisions based on their experience. Teach up-and-coming managers to learn from experience.

- Preach pragmatism: the art of thinking creatively and the practicality of commonsense action steps.

- Encourage employees to think and act pragmatically—that is, to apply good ideas with practical solutions.

CHAPTER 4

TURN PURPOSE INTO GREAT RESULTS

> "The art of being wise is the art of
> knowing what to overlook."
>
> —WILLIAM JAMES, *PRINCIPLES OF PSYCHOLOGY*

Change occurs because people see a better way of doing things and make it happen. Such is the case in the craft beer industry, which brews beer in a traditional way in small batches and with specially selected ingredients—most important, choice hops. One man who seized on the craft beer movement, and in the process helped turn it into something more mainstream, was a triple-degreed Harvard graduate—undergraduate, law, and business. Although he was making good money as a consultant for the prestigious Boston Consulting Group, Jim Koch was a man with beer in his blood. Both his father and grandfather had been brewmasters in his hometown of Cincinnati, Ohio.

With hops "in his veins," so to speak, Koch had something else going for him when he started the Boston Beer Company in 1984: a sense of the audacious. As Sam Hill and Glenn Rifkin write in *Radical Marketing*, Koch balanced his passion for making beer with a passion for talking it up to anyone who would listen. His reputation was not hurt when, six weeks after opening, his company's Samuel Adams brew won the "People's Choice Award" at the Great American Beer Festival in Colorado. Koch parlayed that distinction via an aggressive public relations campaign that got him and his company noticed. In 2010, Koch told the *Wall Street Journal*, "I believe a great beer needs to come from the heart of somebody who really loves it, and you can't fake that."

Koch did more than talk; he also drove a forklift and served as the first brewmaster at Boston Beer, along with full days of selling his beer bar to bar in the Boston area. In time, the demand for craft beers rose, and today it is a multibillion-dollar industry with some 1,500 breweries and millions of loyal beer enthusiasts. Boston Beer Company is one of a handful of craft breweries that have helped educate the palate of beer drinkers, so that they might choose a malt beverage with full flavor, rich taste, and artisan attention to detail.

After more than a quarter century in business, Koch has not lowered his expectations, telling the *Wall Street Journal*, "I want American craft brewing and American beer culture to be recognized all over the world as the epitome of the brewer's art."[1]

Will Koch succeed in that aspiration? Only time will tell. What matters is that his purpose is down to earth: Make great beer that people can enjoy. And in that endeavor he has succeeded. Boston Beer, with a market capitalization of $790 million in 2010, is the premier craft brewery in America.[2]

•   •   •   •   •   •   •

For leadership author John Maxwell, "the greatest motivational principle is people do what people see." Therefore, "the purpose has to be visual."[3] That is, people need to see it and picture it for themselves. The ultimate visualization of purpose in the workplace are the results you achieve. In their groundbreaking book *Built to Last,* Jim Collins and Jerry Porras write that "the primary role of purpose is to guide and inspire."[4] Purpose becomes the impetus for vision because purpose is the sum of your intention, as well as the focus of your energy. Vision, then, is the first step in the translation of your purpose into action.

In my book *How Great Leaders Get Great Results,* I discuss how leaders move their organizations from vision to results. The process begins with a statement of vision. It then ensures that people get behind that vision by giving them ownership in its creation. Once people are on board, you need to do the work. We call this *implementation* or *execution.* The rigor behind firm and steady execution is discipline, which involves holding people accountable for their actions.[5]

Purpose Drives Clarity

In describing purpose, John Maxwell recalls a conversation he had with an executive he had known for some years. The man had achieved much, but was feeling worn out and used up because he had attained all of his goals. Maxwell urged him to get past goals and focus on growth. "You can never maximize growth, but you can maximize goals," he told him.[6] Goals are good for setting direction, but not for sustaining energy. That requires purpose.

You know that a leader radiates purpose when he or she can speak with pride about the organization's products. Dan Denison, of IMD Business School and Denison Consulting, cites the example of an office products CEO who spoke with pride about affinity groups around the country that used his company's products. Another executive for a coffee company believes that in his business it is necessary to hire employees with a passion for the product. By contrast, Denison mentioned an executive in an auto company who confessed that he really was not a "car guy." Although he was nonetheless a fine executive, his lack of passion for his product may have made his role more of a job than a pursuit.[7]

"Establishing purpose is hard work," says Denison. "In a sense, it is akin to climbing a tall mountain." While much energy is expended on strategy and supply-chain dynamics, "thinking about purpose is well worth the time of executives." From purpose flow vision and mission, as well as values. "It is worth focusing on leading for purpose; it has a long life," Dennison concludes.[8]

"I think really good leaders do a superb job of connecting corporate purpose with personal identity," says Tammy Erickson, author and consultant. Such leaders "create a place where I as an individual can take pride and meaning from doing the work." Such an identity can draw strength from competition—that is, from being a member of the winning team, according to Erickson, "because we're building something together that's going to have lasting value or make a difference in some way." Gaining wealth can also be a unifier. Erickson believes that "good leaders shape purpose for their organization in ways that resonate with the individuals who are part of it and help them create personal meaning as well as organizational purpose."[9]

Creating Lasting Engagement

Are you concerned that your workforce cannot adapt to changes facing your organization? You are not alone. According to a 2009 survey of HR professionals by Right Management, nearly one-third (31%) of employees are not adapting, and another 43 percent are coping, but their morale is lagging.[10] As a result, rates of productivity and engagement are declining.

Lower levels of productivity can result from poorly designed systems as well as from a lack of training and resources. Lower levels of engagement can result from a failure to agree on a common purpose. Both are management responsibilities. But although reengineering systems can be time consuming and costly, finding ways to improve engagement does not require costly reengineering; it requires renewed commitment.

Executive coach Marshall Goldsmith notes that while there is much research conducted into how companies engage their employees, there is little research done on how employees engage themselves in work. He illustrates what he means with a story about two flight attendants: "One is positive, motivated, enthusiastic, and gung ho; the other is negative, angry, bitter, and cynical. They're both on the same plane at the same time with the same pay with the same benefits, the same bosses, and the same customers." The difference between the two does not come from outside; it comes from within. The motivated one shares the attitude of a former flight attendant with twenty years' experience who told Goldsmith she enjoyed her job. Her attitude, as she explained, was straightforward. "This is my ministry. I'm going to demonstrate to my passengers what a good person looks like and acts like."[11]

Research that Goldsmith has conducted with his daughter, Kelly, a professor of marketing at Northwestern University, cited in his book *MOJO*, shows that personal engagement with purpose comes with two levers. As Goldsmith explains, "One is a long-term sense of meaning, the sense that I am doing something meaningful. The second is short-term happiness or gratification. I'm doing something that makes me happy." When it comes to long-term meaning, "no one can provide that for you but you." Similarly, when it comes to happiness, "no one can define it for you but you." That said, according to Goldsmith, "leaders can do a much better job of challenging employees by asking, 'All right, how can you make your work more meaningful and purposeful [and] how can you make yourself happier on the job and more engaged?'"[12]

Engagement, true enough, is a buzzword, a favorite of consultants. I think one problem managers have with the concept is that it sounds more like a "flavor of the month" than sound business practice. So, in the interest of clarity, let's break down engagement into two fundamentals: communication and follow-through. You can begin to establish engagement by asking your employees three simple questions:

1. **What is happening?** Sit down with employees one-on-one or in small groups. Have a conversation about what they are doing and how things are going. Do they have what they need to do the job? Do they need more time or more manpower? Simply asking the questions invites discussion. Raising questions about resources does not commit the manager to providing them if they are not available, but it does open the door to determining real needs.

2. **What are you hearing?** Employees often know how well or how poorly things are going. Taking time to listen to what they have to say is critical. Similarly, a good manager wants employees to share what customers are saying about products or what other people in the organization are saying about the work. Such a question tunes a manager in to the grapevine. Some of what employees may share is gossip and may not be true, but a manager needs to know what people inside and outside the organization are thinking, saying, and doing.

3. **What can I do to help?** A manager's job is to support the output. Sometimes her job is to provide resources; sometimes it is to lend a hand with the heavy lifting. Always the manager must be in a position to help the team achieve its objectives. When a manager asks how she can help, she invites discussion and demonstrates that she understands her responsibility to support others. No question could be more fundamental to creating engagement.

Answers to these questions knit communication and follow-through in ways that demonstrate that the leader is interested enough to listen, concerned enough to act, and willing enough to offer assistance.

These activities foster conditions for motivation to flourish. Two presidents, Harry Truman and Dwight Eisenhower, both strongly believed: Leadership comes down to getting people to do what needs doing because they want to do it. Motivation is fundamental to getting others to follow your lead. If you communicate and follow through, you will establish a foundation for motivation, an internal process, to occur.

There is another obstacle to fostering engagement—time, or specifically, the perceived lack of it. So often managers are evaluated—and rightly so—by what they accomplish. However, too many managers have more to do than they can possibly accomplish, and so things like communication and followthrough (and consequently motivation) fall by the wayside. Too bad.

As mentioned, managers work in support of their teams. Their very job is less doing than enabling. The only way they will be able to achieve their objectives is to get the team to pull together and achieve. Managers pitch in as necessary, especially in crunch time, but it is up to managers to guide the process and enable others to achieve. We call that leadership. If you are communicating and following through, you will be demonstrating what it means to engage and ultimately succeed.

Improve Stakeholder Value

Engagement is critical to harnessing the power of employees in an organization so that they, in turn, can focus on what is important to the business and to themselves. To test their engagement, leaders must ask: "What am I doing to drive stakeholder value in our organization? This question arises in the wake of the trashing of the concept of shareholder value. Many financial analysts, belatedly I might add, identify the quest for maximizing shareholder value as a key reason that so many companies took unnecessary risks and assumed high levels of debt in an attempt to grow their businesses in ways that would pump up the share price. As a result, shareholder value has become a kind of pejorative term.

Substitute the word *stakeholder* for *shareholder*, and you have a concept that is holistic because it represents the interests of a broad spectrum. Stakeholders include management, employees, customers, and vendors, as well as shareholders. Local citizens and their governance authorities in communities where businesses reside are also included. Thus, maximizing stakeholder value is a term and concept that any organization can embrace. The challenge becomes how.

Approach to Adding Value

If we assume that value means more than profits and losses, the word *value* (like the word *stakeholder*) takes on greater meaning. It may include everything from product and service performance to how employees feel about their work, to how the organization is perceived by others. Responsibility for ensuring stakeholder value falls to everyone in the organization. In particular, it is a concept that managers who seek to "lead up"—to effect change and achieve positive results—can get behind. There are four questions to ask in this effort:

1. **What are we doing for our customers?** As Peter Drucker taught us, "Customers pay only for what is of use to them and gives them value. Nothing else constitutes quality." Therefore, it is necessary to find out how customers use our products and services, and how we can improve performance as it relates to what customers need: accessibility, affordability, reliability, and utility. Think through what you do to optimize that performance.

2. **What are we doing for our vendors?** Once upon a time, vendors were regarded as nothing more than low-cost providers of whatever the company did not want to make or service itself. Today, supply-chain management involves developing relations with firms whose products and services can make or break your balance sheet. A company and vendor, therefore, have vested interests in each other. Cultivating relationships with vendors is essential not only to optimizing efficiency but also to helping stimulate and incubate innovations that will make your products and services more valuable to your customers.

3. **What are we doing for our employees?** This question can be the game-changer. Ask your employees to consider their colleagues as teammates, each with a vested interest in the welfare and performance of one another. How can they help colleagues do their work more efficiently and, in return, how can they as teammates help you do your work better?

4. **What are we doing to make things better for our community?** Doing well by doing good is nothing new. Companies have always contributed to their communities, but needs continue to escalate. What can businesses contribute to schools or community activities? Individual volunteer efforts are laudable, but companies can work as larger units to find ways of contributing resources that improve the quality of life in the communities in which they operate.

There is one final benefit to improving stakeholder value: It creates higher levels of engagement in the workforce, which, in turn, increase performance. Study after study shows that companies with higher levels of employee engagement financially outperform companies with lower levels of engagement. One reason for this is that engaged workers consider themselves as contributors whose ideas and labor add value to the products and services their companies provide.

Value Validates Purpose

Not only does maximizing stakeholder value make good economic sense, it is an effort in which every employee can participate. The challenge lies in management's communicating what stakeholder value can mean to everyone with a vested interest in the organization. That's not an easy task, but one that can yield strong returns over time.

At Beryl Companies, CEO Paul Spiegelman describes how purpose has been infused into the values proposition, which employees together with management helped develop. The values center on four things: service, quality, ethics, and camaraderie. Over time, those values have become a code of ethics to which employees hold themselves and the company. "They are painted on the wall . . . in big letters in multiple places" all over the office, Spiegelman reports.[13]

Beryl Companies reinforces these values by challenging employees to develop their own personal visions that are based on their values, aspirations, and views toward others. The corporate purpose is "connecting people to healthcare."As Spiegelman explains, "When a call adviser makes some 90 calls a day, and at the end of a seven-minute call receives a reply like, 'God bless you. You really helped me get what I needed today,' then I know that call adviser goes home feeling good about what [he or she] did. That's making the world a better place."[14]

The world is tough and people matter, but you still have to get the work done. So what do leaders need to do to get things done right? Consider how to turn ideas into practicality. We measure the success of an organization by what it achieves; such achievements are a reflection of purpose transformed into action.

Turn Purpose into Great Results: Survey Results

What Employees and Managers Say

Three-fourths of those surveyed believe that leaders can best stimulate innovation and creativity by:

- Identifying what it takes to innovate
- Creating internal think tanks
- Challenging everyone to think creatively
- Rewarding employees for turning ideas into action

Just under two-thirds of respondents believe that leaders could encourage innovation and creativity by providing employees with free time to think.

What Leaders Must Do

Innovation is applied creativity; it is ideas focused on making things better. Anyone in the organization can come up with a good idea, but it is up to management to harness that idea. Therefore, leaders can make it known that ideas are welcome; they are not the sole purview of research and development. "Think time" can be creative time; some organizations give employees time to work on their own projects. Managers can ask their teams to be creative when it comes to problem solving, process improvement, or simply doing things differently. Think tanks are good ideas: These are designated spaces where people engaged on a project can come together to think and talk collaboratively. Creative concepts are only the first step; putting them into action and providing employees with the resources to act upon them are essential. Once employees see their ideas implemented, it stimulates further creativity.

How to Turn Purpose into Great Results

Leadership Questions

- How well do I communicate that I want employees to act as contributors, not as clock punchers?

- How well have I ensured that everyone understands our mission and abides by it?

Leadership Directives

- Hold yourself accountable for results. Let others know how you are progressing on organizational goals. Expect the same of your team.

- Instill discipline throughout the organization; hold people accountable for following agreed-upon processes and procedures.

- Make it known that failure to be accountable—that is, blaming others for your mistakes—is not the way to get ahead.

- Ensure that employees always have the authority to go along with the responsibility to perform their jobs. Communicate who does what and why. Make the lines of reporting crystal clear.

- Give employees the opportunity to create their own job descriptions. Ask managers to work with employees to refine them so that descriptions match the work that needs to be accomplished.

- Cherish employees as contributors—for example, encourage them to add value to the organization. Sometimes this means doing away with the old methods of doing things so that employees have time to focus on what customers really need.

- Tell stories about how the organization has survived hardship. Repeat these stories throughout the organization to boost morale, especially in tough times.

- Adopt a healthy perspective. Specifically compare challenges the organization is facing now with challenges it has faced in the past. Be sure to explain how people in the organization overcame past obstacles and found success.

CHAPTER 5

HOW STRONG PURPOSE MAKES IT SAFE TO FAIL (AS WELL AS TO PREVAIL)

"Fall down seven times, stand up eight times."

—JAPANESE PROVERB

U.S. Congressman Charlie Wilson lived his life so large it would seem natural that it would become a movie. And it did in 2007, in *Charlie Wilson's War,* which centered on the most important aspect of Wilson's political life: providing support to Afghan militia fighting the Soviets in the early 1980s.

Wilson's political consciousness was formed early. His neighbor, a city councilman in his hometown of Lufkin, Texas, killed young Charlie's dog because it would not stop digging in the man's prize flower beds. Thinking big, at least for a youngster, Wilson sought a way to get even with the councilman. Come Election Day, Charlie offered to drive people to the polls, but just before dropping them off, he would tell his passengers, "I don't want to influence your vote, but I'd like you to know that [the councilman] poisoned my dog." The councilman lost by a handful of votes.

That fighting spirit carried Wilson through the Naval Academy (even though he graduated eighth from the bottom of his class), and into a career in politics. He served in the Texas legislature and then was elected to the U.S. House of Representatives.

His grandest venture, and the one captured in the film, was his dogged support to help the Afghan *mujahideen* (opposition groups) repel the Soviet invaders. As he told *Time* magazine, "We were fighting the evil empire." His partner in this venture was a CIA agent, Gus Avrakotos. Wilson used his influence on the Appropriations Committee to fund the effort. The automatic weapons and Stinger missiles, not to mention the mules used to ferry the weapons into Afghanistan after the Soviets killed the Afghani camels, turned the tide. The Soviets pulled out in 1989. Unfortunately, victory was short-lived, as one form of tyranny was replaced by another—the Taliban. Wilson did not regret his mission, but he did regret his inability to get funding to help the Afghani moderates rebuild their infrastructure, schools, and government.[1]

Congressman Wilson was dogged in the pursuit of his mission, which was to expel the Soviets. His purpose was simple: Put a stop to Soviet militant hegemony. He was pragmatic. He was determined. And he was successful.

Doing Something That Matters

Translating purpose into action, and ultimately into results, may be perceived as sequential, but it seldom is. Plans seldom go according to plan; or as General Dwight Eisenhower once said, "In preparing for battle, I have always found that plans are useless, but planning is indispensable."[2] What Ike meant is that the planning process is a creative one; you think of possibilities and then seek to implement them. Reality—in the form of people and processes—intervenes, and the carefully wrought plans get tossed.

All is not lost, however. This is where creativity becomes essential. Leaders must allow their people to flex with changing circumstances. Part of that flexibility involves allowing people to think and do for themselves, giving them the freedom to create alternative ways of doing things to improve their own work as well as the work of others. You can call this innovation, or applied creativity.

Innovation in large organizations is not a solo endeavor. It typically occurs all along the value chain, says Dan Denison of IMD. Denison recalls something that a colleague of his, Dave Robertson, at the Wharton School at the University of Pennsylvania, said about innovation being perceived "as kind of melody, a new tune." For Robertson, innovation is not a melody, it is a chord because "the biggest innovations are happening simultaneously at different places along the value chain in a complementary basis." In this way companies demonstrate innovation in a collaborative way throughout the enterprise.[3]

Another point of resistance to innovation is management's entrenched thinking. As Denison explains, "Hundreds of people can say no and almost nobody can say yes. That means you need to do some political work to get real innovation. That is not only time consuming, it is resource and energy consuming."[4]

Getting Started

Stimulating innovation can be a twofold process, according to Michael Useem, author and professor of management at Wharton. He urges getting outsiders involved, either on the board of directors or as advisers, as "they see the world through different lenses and often have interesting ideas on how to be more efficient or more creative in looking for new kinds of products or services." But it is also important to leverage the talent and skills of people in the ranks. Successful companies like Cisco, Google, and HCL Technologies are good at drawing "creative ideas from people who are most in touch with the market and bringing those ideas up" to senior leadership. In these corporate cultures, Useem explains, employees don't wait to get "innovative ideas from on high"; they do the looking themselves.[5]

Innovation is sometimes perceived as a loaded concept. Whereas most executives say that it is essential, too few are willing to allow their people to take the risks necessary to make it happen. Such hesitancy is understandable. Managers are accountable for results and they need people to do their jobs. Therefore, they fuse the concept of thinking creatively with not getting the work done. This is understandable, but regrettable. So what to do?

Tom Monahan, CEO of the Corporate Executive Board, believes in the power of saying three words: "I don't know." For Monahan, these words do not come from ignorance but from an acknowledgment that management may not have all the answers. It is important to be honest with employees. Make it known that change is inevitable. Pretending that everything will be fine is not acceptable. Faking it with employees will not work; it erodes trust. Being open about what you don't know may not make employees feel comfortable, but they will respect you for admitting it.[6]

Consider innovation not as the development of the next new thing but, rather, the creation of something that will make the current situation better. Certainly a new, well-conceived, and executed product line or service offering that will benefit more than just the bottom line for customers is desirable, but it is not always attainable. What is more realistic is finding ways to work more efficiently and smarter and, in turn, serve customers more effectively. Call this innovation with a small *i*. In other words, you are not seeking to create the next iPhone; you are seeking to create another *i* word—*improvement*.

When you think of improvement, it leads naturally to the concept of pragmatism: practical thinking for practical results. *Pragmatism is purposeful innovation.*

As CEO, Tom Monahan focuses on how to get teams to innovate. As his firm has grown, it has expanded globally. What worked in the past may not work in the future. As Monahan puts it, "We're relatively certain that the next set of things we are going to accomplish will not look like the first set of things we accomplished."[7] Being open to doing things differently is essential.

Innovation is not without risk, but when you take a risk, you need to tell the truth, continues Monahan. This is especially true when asking people to take the lead on a project that may or may not work out. The opportunity is there, but so are the risks. It is necessary to create an environment where "people feel okay being assigned to do difficult things." It is important, says Monahan, to create visibility and generate excitement about the risk venture: "You need to emphasize the learning benefits of taking on certain assignments." Support from senior management is essential because "you don't want to hit the launch and forget it. You spoon-feed resources as necessary." But in case of failure, it is important to remove the stigma of defeat. That is, it was not the executive who failed; it was the company that failed.

After all, it was the company that asked the executive to lead the project. These measures, asserts Monahan, "not only reduce risk but [also enable others] to be comfortable taking a risk."[8]

Innovation is inherently a process of change, and for some employees, that can be hard to take. Henry Ford Health System CEO Nancy Schlichting, who has been in a leadership position in healthcare for 30 years, quoted an employee who asked, " 'Wouldn't it be nice if we didn't have to change anymore?' And I said, 'Well, actually, no, because do you think everything's perfect now?' 'No,' the employee admitted. 'That's why change is needed,' she replied."[9]

Innovation must complement organizational purpose. At the Henry Ford Health System, purpose is rooted in three key drivers: access to quality care, exceptional service, and attention to cost. Knowing these drivers of success provides clarity for employees in the organization. "It will give us short-term financial success . . . and the right results [as well as] keep us relevant and sustained over the long haul," explains Schlichting.[10]

Understanding Risk/Reward

When it comes to risk, Michael Useem of Wharton refers to a "system of enterprise risk management." With such a system in place, typically under the province of a chief risk officer, there is a system of triggers that alert the senior team when too much risk is undertaken. "Having that system in place," says Useem, "allows people the confidence to make calculated judgments on the kind of risks they need to take to make a difference" in the business.[11]

Useem sees risk management best utilized in the U.S. Marine Corps. Marine officers are taught to work with the "70 percent factor." That means that if you are comfortable with 70 percent of your variables, then you can be confident in taking the risk. If you have less than 70 percent, you may be better off taking a pass; but don't wait for 99 percent of the data to arrive because by then it may be too late. The challenge, as the officers are taught, is "not to let perfect be the enemy of getting the job done."[12]

Learning from mistakes is also critical to getting things done. Useem cites a story often told by Charles Elachi, director of NASA's Jet Propulsion Laboratory. When two probes to Mars crashed on impact, the chief engineers of the respective programs offered their resignations. Elachi appreciated their sincerity but replied, "I just spent $400 million for your education on not making that mistake a second time." Instead, Elachi appointed them to head two subsequent missions to Mars, both of which succeeded. Useem concludes that giving people the opportunity to learn from mistakes is essential to risk taking.[13]

When it comes to taking risks, you have to be willing to put your money where your values are. As a CEO, Jim Guest has pushed Consumers Union to be more creative, as well as more entrepreneurial. One year when the company had lost $7 million, Guest pushed the company to spend another million on new ways of marketing in addition to new product development. Fortunately, the risk paid off and the new products, among them the Money Adviser Newsletter, have proved to be profitable.

Guest believes in tapping into the richness of his organization, and to facilitate this, he has instituted "organized brainstorming" sessions. Different teams are challenged to come up with ideas as well as solutions. During the sessions, people are grouped cross-functionally or, as Guest says, into "teams of improbable people"—that is, people who would not normally work together are challenged to do so. Titles are immaterial; ideas are what count. This way, Consumers Union helped break down the silos between functions, and people in different functions shared their expertise with one another.[14]

Innovation requires that "a leader keeps focused on the needs in the marketplace," says Dan Denison of IMD. But that's not the entire story. He recalls Henry Ford's comment that "if he had listened to his customers, they would have asked for a faster horse." Risk is not a safe choice, says Denison, yet the bigger risk lies in doing nothing. Risk taking for a large organization often entails finding ways to protect its own status quo. You cannot wish it so; you need to continue to innovate. As Denison points out, it is imperative to create a business model that is hard for others to implement. For example, both Apple and Google have been able to harness innovation to their business by offering new products that customers want.[15]

Denison notes that one emerging theory of organizations says that companies are essentially "one-trick ponies." They do one thing well and that's it. BlackBerry would be an example. Each of its smartphones is linked to its proprietary data network. While it now offers apps (or applications, a concept pioneered by Apple), it lags far behind. Yet, BlackBerry users tend to buy their instruments for telephony and e-mail, not peripheral computing.

Taking risks can exact penalties. "The economic crash of 2008," notes corporate executive coach Marshall Goldsmith, "was caused by people taking too much risk. There is nothing in risk that is inherently good in and of itself." While Goldsmith allows that some risk is healthy, it is important to put it into perspective. "It is important that people do not take risk with the long-term value of the corporation," especially for short-term gains.[16] That is exactly what many financial institutions did in the years leading up to the crash of 2008. It is therefore important to evaluate risk with questions that get to the heart of the matter: What is the impact of risk on the long-term viability of the corporation? What risks are worth taking and what risks are not worth taking?

"In the military," says Tom Draude, a retired brigadier general and head of the U.S. Marine Corps Foundation, "innovations come normally from junior officers, not senior guys. The junior guys have to be protected so that they can survive when they are raising questions." Some in command positions, including corporate executives, feel threatened by such questions from those below them in rank. They become defensive when questioned, responding with, "This was good enough for me as a first lieutenant, who do you think you are?" The more appropriate response, says Draude, is not to "shoot" the innovator but, rather, to ask "What can we learn?"[17]

"Every leader creates a culture," continues Draude. He used to get a kick out of organizations that called themselves "zero defects" organizations, maintaining that "they must have robots that never break down, because if they have people, there's going to be failure."

People who innovate, admits Draude, are often "pains in the neck and other parts of the anatomy." However, organizations need people who "don't rest on their laurels" but are looking for ways to make things better. One technique that Draude used when he was a corporate executive was to rotate people with potential out of their comfort zones. It did not always work, but Draude believes that to do nothing in the hope of avoiding mistakes is "tantamount to disaster."[18]

Risk Is Uncomfortable

"Most people have an aversion to very much risk," says John Maxwell, a former pastor and founder of his own leadership development company. When talking about risk to his associates and employees, he likes to "catalogue" it. In other words, he likes to place it in the context of what occurred in the past. For example, if the organization took a risk 10 years ago and it worked, it gives the team something to think about. They can perhaps draw confidence from that history if they decide to pursue a new course of action that may have an element of risk. Maxwell says he strives for a "70–75 percent comfort level. I can't hit 10 out of 10, but I'd like to hit about seven out of ten."[19]

Maxwell believes in being honest. He wants his team to know what it did right and what it could have done better. "If you can't be honest about the past, people will not have the security to stretch in the future." And the honesty factor also includes a mention of past accomplishments. "People soon forget the risk but they remember the sweetness of the victory."[20]

When assessing a risk, Maxwell asks three questions:

1. What is the risk?
2. What resources do we need to make it happen?
3. Can we do it?

Such questions give the leader perspective on the risk–reward relationship. By knowing the scope of a project and the resources needed, the leader can make an informed decision. "There have been times," says Maxwell, "when I have felt the risk was too great and I've said, 'We don't want to do this.' In doing so, the leader gains credibility because employees say, 'He's not to going to ask us to do something stupid.' Rather, they will feel, 'He's going to ask us to do something that is a challenge.'"[21]

Driving Innovation

George Reed, a retired Army colonel who teaches leadership at the University of San Diego, identifies several factors that impact creativity, including team composition, individual personalities, motivators, and how the organization functions. "Those conditions can either stimulate or retard the creative inclinations of its people." It falls to the leader to understand these conditions and then to do what is necessary to nurture a more creative atmosphere.

"Look at the organizations that are the most creative. They tend to be playful. They tend to be places where people laugh a lot," reflects Reed. Employees can have fun. "They also need to be able to laugh at themselves," says Reed, because failure can be tough. "Leaders have to control their emotions and their behaviors in the face of performance that does not meet their expectations. If they act inappropriately, it will certainly quash creativity and innovation."[22]

Innovation within the Henry Ford Health System in Detroit, Michigan, is part of its DNA. When he created the hospital that bore his name in 1915, founder Henry Ford promoted the concept of salaried physicians, as well as academics, in medicine. Yet innovation is nothing new. Today, CEO Nancy Schlichting believes in taking nothing for granted: "It's so typical for leaders when people come up with new ideas that don't necessarily align with the strategy of today to say 'no.' And my belief is you have to say 'yes.'"[23]

Words are only a door opener. Two examples of innovation at Henry Ford have attracted wide notice. The first was the decision to invest $13 million for an operating theater with robotic instruments for prostate surgery. "It was an experiment," says Schlichting, and it worked. To date, the Vattikuti Urology Institute, featuring robotic prostatectomy pioneered by Dr. Mani Menon, has treated patients from all 50 states and every continent in the world.

A more bold experiment was Schlichting's decision to hire Gerard van Grinsven to be CEO of a proposed new hospital in West Bloomfield, a suburb of Detroit. Van Grinsven had no experience in healthcare; he was an executive with Ritz-Carlton, and he had spent his entire career in hotel administration. It was a risk, but one that was hedged by van Grinsven's track record of opening successful hotels, as well as his exemplary history of leadership in creating a culture of service. Yet, as Schlichting puts it, "My chief operating officer at the time thought I had lost my mind."[24]

Schlichting wanted van Grinsven to establish a new approach that would combine the service ethos of a fine hotel with the commitment to healthcare that already distinguished Henry Ford Hospital. The risk paid off; since its opening in 2009, Henry Ford Hospital West Bloomfield has established itself as a first-rate medical facility with a holistic approach to medicine that emphasizes treatment, prevention, and wellness. "I've raised service to an entirely new level, [and] it requires identifying leaders who have service in their hearts, have a passion for it," summarizes Schlichting.[25]

Risk taking is not solely a leadership proposition. Employees who are willing to innovate put their careers on the line, too. "You have to have thick skin on the part of the risk-taker and the risk-giver," concludes Schlichting. Leaders investing in risk need to have guts, resiliency, and the courage to stand up to naysayers.

Understanding Setbacks

Failure is part of business. Within the culture of Beryl Companies, taking risks is accepted. The challenge, explains CEO Paul Spiegelman, is how you react when things go wrong. What Spiegelman strives to do is ask the question, "What did we learn and how do we move forward?" not "Who do we blame?"

Spiegelman's methodology for dealing with mistakes is "to pull the group together and have us all self-reflect" on what happened and why. Experience indicates that, most often, mistakes occurred for the best of intentions. Employees thought they were doing the right thing, but the situation deteriorated for reasons beyond their control. Spiegelman maintains that, though diagnosing why things went wrong is important, so too is "how you deal with it that lets people know that it's okay to make a mistake," as long as there is learning and a resolution to do better the next time.[26]

While levels of trust between senior leadership and employees in large organizations may be eroded, Spiegelman asserts that this is not the case with smaller businesses like his. He gives three reasons for this. The first is transparency—in particular, open-book management. "We share the financial details of our company freely and openly with everyone in the company." But that's not all. "We educate people on what [the numbers] mean." The second reason is accountability, which extends to every level in the company from the bottom to the top.[27]

The third reason is personal commitment to employees that supports them outside the workplace. An example is something the company calls "Beryl Cares," which endeavors to recognize the personal lives of employees in good times and bad. It is a way for employees to share milestone achievements, as well as the loss of health or a loved one. The program also allows the company to support employees financially if they are out of work for an extended period of time. This contribution is over and above healthcare costs, which are covered through insurance.

Employees are also welcome to pitch in and help one another in times of need, often with bake sales and car washes. Spiegelman recalled one man who didn't want employees doing anything special for him, because he knew that many were single mothers and might have had a hard time contributing. As Spiegelman says, the man told him that he didn't want to be in a position of "taking money away from what they could use for their own kids." That sentiment only affirms the company's commitment to helping its employees.

The culture at Beryl Companies can be quantitatively measured via employee engagement surveys. Over the past five years, in a time when trust levels have been eroding in industries as a whole, employees at Beryl have been ever more engaged. Spiegelman is pleased, but not totally satisfied. The low scores serve as targets for the following year.

But employee engagement scores are not mere bragging points for Spiegelman; there is a solid business case behind them. Beryl Companies has grown revenues by double digits and profits by triple digits. Profitability also exceeds that of its competitors, despite the fact that, as Spiegelman points out, "we're 40 percent more expensive than our next closest competitor." Premium pricing, as Spiegelman puts it, only works when employees are engaged in the work and produce results that satisfy or exceed customer expectations.[28]

Creating such strong engagement relies upon a principle that Spiegelman describes as the "circle of growth." It begins with employee loyalty, which in turn drives customer loyalty. "If your customers are loyal, that will drive profitability," Spiegelman asserts. As a private company, Beryl can turn its profits back to its people, "giving them better tools and resources to do their jobs" as well as competitive wages and benefits.[29]

The Virtue of Pragmatism

Pragmatism is the engine of innovation. While it relies on creativity for its spark, it is ingenuity that turns ideas into practical concepts. That requires a *sense* of pragmatism, particularly in terms of what works and what does not. No company will succeed all of the time, but they all need to allow their workforces to experiment. Reasonable risk is necessary to survival, and so failure must be an option. Adhering to the organization's purpose can provide the inspiration for innovation, as well as the support for taking risks.

When it comes to taking risks, George Reed, of the University of San Diego, advises an approach that incorporates learning. He explains that there must be "some tolerance of mistakes, because we know that most experiments fail and most big ideas don't meet their initial expectations." Without that understanding, he adds, "there is no possibility for the organization to learn. The trick is tolerating mistakes in the name of learning and not tolerating suboptimal performance" that could harm the organization. There is also the balance between what Reed calls prudence and timidity—in short, "know what you can risk and no more."[30]

Leaders can make innovation more acceptable by "asking interesting questions," says Tammy Erickson, author and consultant. While the perception is that leaders must set direction, Erickson would like to see leaders "ask questions that will engage people and get them excited" about the possibilities. It is important to set goals and have targets, but sometimes such targets can be limiting. By contrast, says Erickson, "An interesting question rather than a numerical target can free people's minds."[31]

Erickson, who specializes in researching and writing about generational issues, also believes that leaders can make ambiguity tolerable by linking purpose to people. Work that Erickson has done in her consulting practice reveals that people share ideas and innovate when they have "relationships that are trust based." For example, explains Erickson, "if you are expecting your marketing and R&D departments to collaborate, you have to stop and consider whether [individuals] actually know each other as people." Leaders must help foster those person-to-person relationships. They can do this by facilitating introductions, and also by holding leaders of different teams accountable for making personal connections.[32]

It is also important, says Erickson, to "ensure that your people have access to disruptive ideas. With an insular and static organization, you're not going to get innovation. People have to have the fresh air of provocative thinking and new ideas." Leaders can do this in a number of ways, according to Erickson. They can insist that their people keep up-to-date on trends affecting their business, attend conferences, and continue their professional development. Staging off-sites with industry experts is a good way to present new ideas. It may even make sense for leaders to invite people from outside their field to speak to their people. Having a physicist lecture on string theory or a musical group conduct a music appreciation class may not be germane to the business at hand, but it does stimulate people to think about the world around them in new and different ways. Adopting new perspectives is essential to innovation.[33]

Is Your Culture Holding Your Good Ideas Back?

"How do you innovate if you work in a culture that won't let you be creative?" That question, which came from a student in one of my workshops, hit me with the metaphorical punch to the solar plexus. You see, those of us in the consulting profession are forever urging our clients, in whatever organizations they work, to "be more creative," to "adopt a new paradigm," or to "think outside of the box." Well, if you work in an environment that values rules over thought, your paradigm *is* the box; thinking outside of it (even peering over the top of it) is nigh on impossible.

Or is it? Recovering my breath, I turned to the questioner and said something like, "Invite your people to share their ideas with you; that is, adopt the open-door/open-mind outlook." Make it known that you welcome ideas. Likely, the most creative people in your organization are either the front-liners—because they often deal most directly with customers—or the new hires, because they come to the organization (you hope) with an attitude that is more upbeat than downbeat (in other words, they haven't yet been corrupted by a culture that says, "No new ideas wanted!").

At UCO, innovation has become a means of coping with change, and it's why, says President Roger Webb, "we've become known as a pretty innovative and creative university." For universities to survive, he continues, "we've got to find ways to have an environment that encourages creative thought." Do it not with words but with actions. UCO has a creative council composed of faculty and staff where lunch is served and ideas are exchanged. "We dream together," Webb explains. There is also the creativity room, open every afternoon where a sign overhead proclaims, IDEAS WELCOME. The creativity room, equipped with smart technologies such as an electronic whiteboard, is open to groups to come in and brainstorm.[34]

Webb fervently believes that ideas need to be nurtured, and so the university awards $2,000 grants to individuals and groups who come up with new and different ways of dealing with issues every university faces, such as class scheduling, parking, and even insect problems. These are not breakthrough concepts, but the cash incentives communicate that the university wants to improve and is willing to reward people for their good ideas.

While Webb prides himself on fostering a culture that values ideas, he knows he is fighting an uphill battle. When it comes to innovation, Webb knows more about stifling it than nurturing it: "We kill ideas as presidents because of the fear of being wrong." There is also a real fear of embarrassment within academia, he admits.[35]

Webb recounts how one idea that he proposed blew up because, although the concept was valid, the execution was poor. UCO is the state's number one producer of teachers. Since the charter school and the online education movements are growing, the university decided to sponsor one of each. The online provider with whom UCO contracted proved to be less than trustworthy and the resulting publicity reflected poorly on the university. Owning up to the mistake is important, says Webb, and it will not kill the creative process. In short, you don't throw good ideas away because of poor execution if the reason you pursued them is integral to your organizational mission. Experimentation is critical to innovation and failures will occur.

Risk does have its rewards, though. One that has paid off handsomely for UCO is its School of Rock. Though UCO has long had a school of music, it realized that it was missing students who were interested in pursuing music as a career, but who could not qualify academically for the university. The university partnered with the Academy of Contemporary Music based in the United Kingdom to offer a similar program in Oklahoma City, 20 miles from UCO's campus in Edmund. Being in the city proved to be ideal because of its emerging cultural scene, and the School of Rock was designed to attract students looking for education in music as well as the music business. The school opened in August 2009 with 150 students, then added another 100 the following January. Enrollment is now (in 2011) at 500.

Not only was there financial risk involved in converting an old building in Oklahoma City to house the School of Rock, but there also was academic risk. Webb pushed the board to admit applicants as community college students, for which entrance requirements were less rigorous. Additionally, the board approved the hiring of faculty who were working professionals rather than academics. At the same time, the school integrated its general education courses to supplement the music curriculum. This way, students graduate with an associate's degree as well as certification from the Academy of Contemporary Music, which is useful for those who want to pursue music professionally. Graduates also qualify for admission to a four-year university to complete their undergraduate degrees.

The School of Rock has generated favorable publicity for UCO, and when big-name touring professionals come to Oklahoma City for concerts, some drop by the school to teach a class. What's more, President Webb brags that, since the school is part of a public university, it is competitively priced, costing a fraction of what a similar musical education might cost at private university.

Methods for Stimulating Innovation

Research shows that creativity is the lifeblood of any organization. Yet creativity cannot exist in a vacuum. It must be nurtured by a culture that values it, and it must be developed by managers who understand it. W. L. Gore and Associates, Inc., maker of Gore-Tex, is one such company. They are so innovative that employees do not have titles or even job descriptions. They gravitate to projects they like, and if the team agrees, they join; if not, they move on (or out of the company).

Now this example is an extreme, but the U.S. Marine Corps is another organization that values innovation—most especially where it matters. They adopt new technology as well as new tactics in order to become more adept at outwitting and outmaneuvering the enemy. Their goal is to keep the troops safer when they are in harm's way. Doing that requires a flexible and creative mindset.

Understanding that creativity is vital to business is essential, and so it falls to line managers, often those in the middle who want to make changes, to make the first move. To do that, they need to adopt a more innovative mindset themselves. Here are some suggestions for doing so:

• **Listen to the grapevine.** So often, companies that communicate from the top down miss out on the most dynamic form of communication in the organization: what people talk about in the hallways or in the break room. Call it the grapevine—it is where you feel the pulse of what's happening, or what's not happening. Leaders who want to nurture innovation need to tune in to it. How? By visiting the haunts of the grapevine talkers and just listening.

As a manager, you have to make it safe for people to speak to you, and especially to tell you what you don't want to hear. Their gripes—whether about a boss, a process, or a system—are good indicators of what is holding people back, often keeping them from thinking creatively. For instance, they are spending more time in frustration than in creation. That's an unhealthy sign. Managers need to bust those roadblocks, and bust 'em good, if they are to allow creativity to flourish. Or as gifted comedian John Cleese says, "If you want creative workers, give them enough time to play."

- **Anyone can be creative.** Consultant/author Nancy Austin makes a wonderful case for innovation in her keynote presentations. One telling story she relates is about the variety of designs found even in the most humble of household objects—the toilet bowl brush. Such brushes come in all shapes, sizes, and colors, as well as prices befitting toilets made of marble or gold! Austin's point is straightforward: If you can be innovative with a toilet brush, then you can be creative in just about any other endeavor. Innovation does not require a home run—a breakthrough product or concept. For example, engineers may simply remove a step from a process, front-liners may take a new approach to service, or marketers can offer new ideas to project teams. What is required is management that understands the value of people who play with innovation.[36]

- **Look at your customer.** Many companies innovate from the bottom up. That push upward comes from frontline people as well as customers. Together they make a potent force for change. For example, the domestic automotive industry discovered customer service, something that companies like Mercedes-Benz had long delivered and Lexus and Infiniti had developed to a high art. American companies like Ford and GM started asking their customers what they expected, and the companies revamped sales and service practices in dealerships to accommodate those demands. Left to their own devices, the domestic companies might not have bothered; but by listening to retail customers (us) and wholesale customers (dealers), they innovated. It was not revolutionary, but it was a break from the past that met customer needs.

- **Study your competition.** Picture yourself standing on the highway. All of a sudden, a large vehicle comes out of nowhere and whizzes past, so fast that it musses your hair and ruffles your clothes.

That's the sensation felt by folks working for companies that are by-passed by their competitors. In the IT world, this sensation is part and parcel of doing business. The good news is that great innovations for many companies are often just around the proverbial bend, in the form of a new piece of hardware, software, or netware. Looking at the competition is a good impetus for innovation. The trick is not to become mesmerized by what you see, however. Look beyond what the competitor is doing to determine the next wave. That's where the true innovators belong.

Make a Move

All of these steps are essential to effective innovation, but some organizations, for whatever reasons—misunderstanding, fear, or lack of concern—want no part of doing things differently. Managers who live in that kind of system then have two choices: shut up and plod along, or leave. The former is an insufferable option for many, and so the latter may be the better course. Many an entrepreneur got his or her start by working in a large organization that did not permit new ideas. Tired of consistent rejection, they left and began their own businesses. The world is better for such folks, be they Ray Kroc of McDonald's or James Power III of J. D. Power and Associates. Each created a business that provides a product or service that consumers value, and each employs many other people. That's an example of applied creativity.

Innovation is essential. It is the differentiator between successful companies and fence-sitters. Yet it cannot be taken for granted. The truly creative will leave; the so-so creative will remain, but their ideas will go nowhere. So it becomes the job of the manager, as leader, to step forward and champion good ideas, along the way recognizing those doing the creating. "Creativity is so delicate a flower that praise tends to make it bloom," wrote advertising executive Alex Osborn, "while discouragement often nips it in the bud. Any of us will put out more and better ideas if our efforts are appreciated."[37] When this happens, the question about creativity in an uncreative workplace becomes moot—and happily so.

How Strong Purpose Makes It Safe to Fail: Survey Results

What Employees and Managers Say

Over 85 percent of those surveyed believe leaders can encourage employees to take risks and show them that it is integral to success by:

- Challenging employees to think outside the box
- Creating internal think tank–style incubators
- Rewarding employees for taking risks
- Providing clear guidance of strategic direction
- Recognizing people who overcome job challenges

What Leaders Must Do

Not all risks are worth taking, and management can set parameters about what level of risk is acceptable. However, taking risks is essential to innovation. Projects do not always unfold in an expected fashion, so risk is inherent in any endeavor. Teaching people to accept some risk is essential to proper management. Guidance is critical; risk must be linked to strategic imperatives. Incubators for evaluating risks can be a means for people to assess the level of risk. Those who take risks and achieve results need to be recognized, just as those who risk and fail need to be encouraged to continue to try as long as what they are attempting complements the organizational mission.

How to Make It Safe for People to Create and Innovate

Leadership Questions

- How well do I set the tone for accepting creative ideas?

- What more can I do to make it safe for people to collaborate creatively?

Leadership Directives

- Integrate brainstorming sessions into at least one staff meeting per month.

- Draw a distinction between accountability and creativity. Accountability is the courage to stand up for what you do. Creativity is the courage to try something different. Organizations need both to survive.

- Encourage people to think about how they can do their jobs better. Make it clear to managers that you expect employees to voice new ideas. That does not mean all ideas need to be accepted or implemented, but it does mean that managers need to encourage people to speak up when they have a good idea.

- Recognize employees who find ways to improve the customer experience.

- Consider staging an off-site to stimulate creativity at least once per year. The off-site should include brainstorming sessions as well as opportunities to develop new ideas. Invite outside guests from different walks of life. The stories they tell may help your people think of new possibilities based on what they learn from others.

- Suggest that employees look outside their industry for good ideas in areas related to their function—for example, finance, human resources, marketing. Encourage employees to attend conferences related to their functions so they can keep themselves abreast of new developments in their field.

CHAPTER 6

DEVELOP THE NEXT GENERATION OF PURPOSEFUL LEADERS

> "I am convinced that nothing we do is more important than hiring and developing people. At the end of the day you bet on people, not on strategies."
>
> —LARRY BOSSIDY, BUSINESSMAN AND AUTHOR

Once upon a time they called him the "Indiana Rubber Man" because he was so agile. Much later, they called him the "Wizard of Westwood," as well as the "Reverend." Of these monikers, the one he despised was "Wizard" because, in his mind, there was no magic to what he did. He was a teacher who became the most successful coach—at least in terms of championship titles—in collegiate basketball history. He was John Wooden.

A coach in high school, and later in college for more than 40 years, Wooden left a legacy not in wins and losses, which were impressive, but in the boys he schooled on the court to act like men off of the court. Born in 1910 in a small town in Indiana, Wooden eventually ended up in one of America's most vibrant cities, Los Angeles; but he never lost that hometown sense of purpose: Righteous living leads to righteous results. Jim Murray, famed *Los Angeles Times* columnist, once wrote that when you met Wooden, you could "smell the hay if you close[d] your eyes."

But Wooden was no hayseed. He took his mission seriously. As he told the *New York Times,* he strove to teach three things to his players: conditioning, "quickness," and teamwork. That was on the court. Off the court, he preached (and that is the most appropriate verb) the "pyramid of success," a collection of life's principles learned from his father and honed over the years through his own experience. He truly was a teacher interested not simply in how well his players performed on the court but also how well they comported themselves off of it.

True enough, not all the players bought into this philosophy; some thought he was out of touch. But as one player once commented, all those lessons came back to him once he had children of his own. This is something about which one of UCLA's greatest players, Bill Walton, waxes frequently.

Wooden never cut his players any slack. Once, during the time of U.S. involvement in the Vietnam War, the players wanted to cut practice to attend an antiwar rally. Wooden, according to *Sports Illustrated,* inquired about their sincerity, then assured them "that he had his convictions, too, and if they missed practice, that would be the end of their careers at UCLA."

Discipline was the spine of Wooden's beliefs. He did recruit great talent, but he also developed that talent to perform as a single unit: "You'd better play together or you sit" was his frequent admonition to them before a game. When Wooden died in 2010, the outpouring of remembrances from fellow coaches and players was testimony to the impact that he had had on the game and on others. Though always a modest man, he would have smiled if he knew he was remembered not simply as one who got his teams to win but also one who taught his players lessons that would last them a lifetime.[1]

•   •   •   •   •   •   •

Few senior business leaders will be in their current jobs five or ten years from now. They may be heading other organizations or they may have retired. So who will be in charge? That is the question that every leader must ask every day. But it's not enough to pose the question. The challenge becomes one of preparing your people for the future. A purposeful leader's legacy lies within the next generation of leaders. When they know the purpose, and deliver on it, then the organization has the opportunity to succeed over the long term.

Who's on Deck?

Grooming the next generation of leaders, or, as corporate executive coach Marshall Goldsmith prefers to call it, "succession development," should be part of every leader's job description. According to Goldsmith, whose book *Succession: Are You Ready?* deals with the topic extensively, "every leader should have people being prepared for the succession process."[2] Succession planning is a matter of putting names into the boxes of an organization chart; succession development is about preparing people for higher levels of responsibility. Toward that end, it is important to look at more than "the next CEO"; it also involves looking "at the next two or three generations who could be CEO."[3]

One way to gauge leadership development is to measure it. Goldsmith cites the example of one company that did this by including the question, "How many people got promoted from your organization?" into its performance-appraisal process. Part of the appraisal also asked, "What's being done to develop these people and how can you document their developmental process?" In this way, the company was able to document how well managers were developing and promoting their direct reports.[4]

Pat Williams, who was a professional baseball player before going into sports management, knows the value of judging talent. Now senior vice president of the Orlando Magic, he has been active in the NBA for decades. Williams traded for Julius Erving, Moses Malone, and Deon "Penny" Hardaway.[5] He also drafted Charles Barkley and Shaquille O'Neal. On the management side, Williams signed Chuck Daly to his first professional coaching contract. Daly is the only coach ever to win an Olympic Gold medal (Team USA 1992) and an NBA championship (Detroit Pistons).

Williams says, "Your scouts are making some very bold decisions. And they are not all going to work. But if a scout feels that past mistakes are held against him, he will not take any more risks. He's going to play it safe." As a result, the team for whom the scout works will lose out on future talent. Williams therefore urges leaders to allow risk taking to avoid mediocrity. "We are a bold, aggressive organization," says Williams. "We have big goals. We know playing it close to the net is not going to get us there."[6]

"You've got to give people the freedom to be creative and imaginative," Williams continues. "There has to be an atmosphere that risk taking is good. It is important to nurture the feeling: I want all of your ideas. No one is going to laugh at you, mock you, or scorn you." Unfortunately, the opposite is more often true. "There's the sense of fear and of insecurity," Williams notes, which engenders the feeling that it's better to keep one's ideas to oneself because "'no one listens to me.'" Williams admires the "blue sky thinking approach" practiced by Walt Disney and carried out by his company to this day. Brainstorming can lead to great ideas.[7]

Thinking About Talent

Leaders need to be prepared to handle good talent. "Talented people can be very creative," says Pat Williams. "They can be very imaginative. They have minds of their own. They could be original in their thinking. And there are many organizations that are absolutely terrified of that."[8]

A much-in-demand keynote speaker, Williams believes that "senior leaders have to understand that as they get older and more mature, a huge part of their job is getting the next generation below them ready to take the baton into their own hands." Williams cites a conversation with Howard Shultz, founder and CEO of Starbucks, a company that has a tradition of promoting managers from within the ranks, making it truly in the "people business." Schultz, like many other successful entrepreneurs, realizes that his company is only as good as the people it hires and the leaders it develops.[9]

John Maxwell, who has devoted much of his career to teaching and writing on the subject, argues that leadership "is not a three-month teaching series. It's a culture thing, a way of life. It's everyone growing as a leader." Maxwell recalls a conversation he had with legendary General Electric CEO Jack Welch about his company's succession process. Welch reported that GE did not look for specific leaders for specific spots; rather, it sought out leaders who knew how to lead and were capable of adapting to emerging new realities. Maxwell agrees with that philosophy, saying, "You don't develop leaders because you need someone to take your place. You develop leaders because you need better leaders at every strata and every level." It is a matter of creating a leadership culture, and the stronger that is, "the more possibility you have to develop those who can rise up within your organization."[10]

Michael Useem has also spent much of his professional life teaching leadership to men and women in many different disciplines, chiefly through his work as a professor at the University of Pennsylvania's Wharton School of Business. He has written a number of books and done a significant amount of research on the topic as well. Useem asserts that, "Leadership is not a natural skill set." He adds, "A few people seem to have it from their early years, but for most people, it is something mastered later in life. Thus, I am a strong proponent of organizations creating explicit leadership development programs to bring that next generation along."[11]

According to Useem, three factors are necessary for success in leadership development. First, employees have to be encouraged to become "self-directed students of leadership on a lifelong basis." This will make them "adept at watching good bosses and bad bosses, [and] looking at each as a lesson or set of lessons from which they can learn how to be good at this sport." Second, the organization has to "provide people with coaches and mentors. It is important to offer finely honed, actionable feedback." Doing it off-line gives the opportunity for one-to-one conversations about performance and the quest for improvement. The third factor is "to give people increasing opportunities to do what they've not done before." Increasing levels of responsibility progressively gives emerging leaders the opportunity to acquire new skills, particularly in decision making.[12]

When it comes to delivering on purpose, Useem believes it is something that is communicated best by example. Whatever the mission of a company, the leader fulfills it by voicing it repeatedly. Useem suggests that you both "begin and conclude every meeting with a reference to your ultimate mission."[13]

As far as finding the next generation of leaders, Michelle Rhee, former Chancellor of the Washington, D.C., public school district, says, "I'm very good at sniffing out talent." She looks for the best and brightest. "I like to surround myself with people who are way better, way smarter at doing what they do than I could ever be." Her role then becomes "to block and tackle for those folks." With that kind of talent on the management team, believes Rhee, it is possible to "build the right kind of skills for the next level of leadership."[14]

Discovering talent begins with an interview. Rhee likes to ask candidates how they realized they were successful. If they respond that their bosses told them so, Rhee gives them a pass. But if they quantify their success in terms of metrics and goals, Rhee shows interest. Communication skills are important, but so too are people who are unconventional thinkers. "I look for people who are stand-up leaders," says Rhee. She defines that term as "someone who's going to take accountability and responsibility regardless of how things are going."[15]

Five Salient Elements in Successful Leadership Development Programs

While leadership development efforts sometimes wane during financial belt tightening, they really do not disappear, as evidenced by research by *Bloomberg/BusinessWeek* and the Hay Group in 2010.[16] Yet the experience of the most significant financial crisis since the Great Depression should not be lost. It is worth debating the merits of these programs. Specifically, if our leadership programs were so good, why did so many businesses suffer?

Failure of leadership is a prime culprit. Senior executives in many companies put short-term gain ahead of long-term sustainability, and as a result, many businesses, especially those in the automotive and financial sectors, suffered catastrophic losses. Just as business schools are revamping their curricula to prepare students for the new realities and mandates of tomorrow—with more emphasis on ethics and sustainability, as well as on critical thinking—the practitioners of leadership development should do the very same. Here are five points that I have gleaned from my observations and participation in successful leadership development efforts:

1. **Capacity: What do I know about myself?** Self-awareness is essential to leadership. Helping a leader gain a better picture of his or her strengths and growth opportunities is critical. One way to help participants understand themselves is through the assessment process, which can be a combination of standardized self-assessments and 360-degree evaluations. The latter can give a good picture of how the leader is perceived by others, which is fundamental to true self-knowledge.

2. **Competency: What does it take to be a leader in my organization?** Many organizations spend a great deal of time and energy considering the behaviors necessary to lead, as well as the values such leaders must possess. The coupling of behaviors with values sets expectations for leaders to be honest and ethical, as well as puts them on notice that they need to treat others as they would wish to be treated. (Yes, the Golden Rule.)

3. **Challenges: What is holding us back from achieving our goals?** Now it's time for a reality check. Good leadership programs are those that address the roadblocks an organization is facing. Such roadblocks may be cultural (no one communicates), managerial (no competence), lack of direction (no vision), or failure to execute (no consistency). Addressing these real-world issues in the context of a training program is vital to credibility, as well as for preparing people to deal with adversity.

4. **Solutions: How can we solve problems facing the organization?** This is thinking-cap time. Innovation is essential to growth, but innovation may also be applied to solving problems. Programs that stimulate critical thinking as well as creativity are those that broaden the definition of leadership beyond merely guiding followers to include solving problems that hinder or prevent professional and organizational development.

5. **Opportunities: What results can we achieve by demonstrating leadership?** It is important to challenge participants to think about what they can do to effect positive change in their organizations. Small changes may include shifts in behavior that make them better communicators, delegators, and supervisors. Big changes may include ways to change the culture, so that their organizations are more responsive to customer needs; such a change would require more frontline leadership and better listening from those in positions of power.

Accelerate the Learning Curve

The single best way to reinforce these five points for leadership development is through action learning. This principle lies at the core of how our military develops its next generation of leaders, both commissioned and noncommissioned. You learn by doing.

Leadership development works best if it can accelerate the learning process. One approach that CEO Jim Guest of Consumers Union used was to include young managers on his leadership team. Annually, two or three emerging leaders with 10 to 12 years of professional experience would rotate onto the committee and stay for a year. Guest maintains that this gave the younger managers insight into what was happening at the strategic level and taught them how decisions were made. They also participated in leadership discussions and engaged in the decision-making process. Membership on this committee created a cadre of future leaders that Guest could draw upon for special projects or initiatives.[17]

Tom Monahan, CEO of the Corporate Executive Board, is candid about his leadership development, stating, "You're hurting yourself in two places when you don't give someone the [broader] breadth of responsibility they need to have to be a fully fledged leader. One, you pull them out of what they excel at doing. Two, you put them on a learning curve in a new position." Therefore, according to Monahan, an organization must have "a tolerance for risk to put people in roles where they are challenged and stretched. There will be bumpiness along the way that creates fuller fledged, richer leaders."[18]

The Corporate Executive Board invests heavily in training. But the biggest benefit may not be in the tangible skills acquired in the classroom but, rather, in the experience of "getting people from different parts of the business together so they forge relationships that they carry over outside of the classroom." Training, Monahan adds, then becomes "lateral networks for people . . . the ability to have a great peer network at work really helps people round out their understanding of the business." Such a network helps people innovate because "they can reach out, they get sounding boards" from their peer network.[19]

Leadership development at the Corporate Executive Board involves senior leaders. It has developed something it calls "diagonal networks" that enable leaders in one function to spend time mentoring employees in another function. The benefits are twofold, explains Monahan, when "people feel multiple sponsors at the top of the house." As a result, they feel they belong to the company, not simply the function. The other benefit is that employees get a close-up view "of some of the decisions the whole leadership team makes, providing a perspective that is not possible when working at only one level, in one function."[20]

Such "diagonal networking" further stimulates individual employee development in two ways, adds Monahan. First, employees gain more technical expertise—"resources to draw on to solve everyday problems." Second, they gain insight into the leadership perspectives of people other than their bosses. As Monahan says, "My direct reports know most of my tricks." So he encourages them to reach out to other leaders to see how they might size up a situation.[21]

In the corporate environment, businesspeople put into practice what they learn in the classroom. Projects may be internal business-development initiatives—that is, developing a business plan and implementing it for a project or a process to be initiated. Such efforts may also be directed to the community; for example, doing something that benefits a local school system or community service initiative. Whatever the project, the challenge is for leaders to put into practice what they have learned about themselves, as well as what they have learned about their capacity to lead others. However, action learning does not preclude classroom-style programs. Teaching begins in the classroom, but if leadership is to take hold, participants must practice what they learn.

The Beryl Companies provides career paths for its employees and supports them with training and leadership development programs. But as the company has grown, it has also brought in talent from the outside, which has sometimes caused disgruntlement. As Beryl CEO Paul Spiegelman explains, you have to be honest with people by telling them, "The worst thing we could do would be to give you a title, give you no tools and resources to succeed, and then blame you in three years when things are not working out." What employees need are experienced mentors who will help them grow in the organization and who will remind them, "It's not a threat to you. It's an opportunity."[22]

Finally, it's important to understand that leadership is a choice. We choose to become leaders; it is that choice that enables us to do what is necessary for the organization to succeed. Sacrifice, in the form of giving of oneself, is essential, but you cannot make a leader of someone who does not want that. The decision to become a leader is personal. Leadership development efforts strive to open the doors to what leadership truly is so that people can make the right choice for themselves and their organizations.

Making Time to Teach Emerging Leaders

Leadership development is a matter of commitment. As a retired career officer, George Reed has a bias for the way the U.S. military develops its leaders. He believes that many of its practices are applicable to civilian life, and he lives out this belief every day in his position as professor at the University of San Diego. One fundamental, says Reed, is to have a "common lexicon for leadership." In the military, soldiers can refer to the field manual to discover roles and responsibilities for each rank. Some organizations seek to replicate the principles of the field manual with a leadership competency roadmap that specifies what it means to be a leader in the organization. The more clarity there is concerning leadership, the more likely it will be undertaken.[23]

The military, according to Reed, does a good job of training leaders, from noncommissioned to commissioned officers. There is a school for each rank, "a system of professional military education to the assignment process," explains Reed. "If you're going to be a general officer, you're going to go the U.S. Army War College. No exceptions." In his consulting work with businesses or other nonmilitary organizations, Reed suggests that they consider "transition points"— that is, points at which leaders move from individual contributors to team leaders, managers, functional managers, and general managers through the leadership pipeline. Some organizations do a good job of preparing employees for each step in such a process. (Noted consultant Ram Charan, together with Stephen Drotter and James Noel, wrote a book on this very topic entitled *Leadership Pipeline*.[24]) As Reed reiterates, driving for clarity at each step in the leadership process prepares leaders to know what is expected of them. Such clarity sets a foundation of knowledge upon which a leader can grow.[25]

Reed employs another concept borrowed from the military for optimizing leadership development in the corporate sector: Pay for it through a centralized funding source. In most organizations, the function (marketing, finance, operations) pays for its own employee development. Reed sees this as a disincentive, arguing, "If you decide not to send someone" through a leadership course, you save "money in your budget that you can use for others things." By contrast, with centralized funding, leadership development is enterprise-wide. As Reed notes, "There's always an incentive to spend someone else's money."[26]

Finally, the goal of leadership development, according to Reed, should not be that of creating a school or course. Rather, the intention should be to create "a culture of leadership development where everyone is preparing for the next level of responsibility, or at least thinking about how to bring the next person along."[27]

As necessary as it is to innovate in products and services, it may also be necessary to innovate inside your organization. Paul Spiegelman, CEO of the Beryl Companies, says that sometimes you need to "challenge the purpose . . . or the mission of the organization." This is an issue that the Beryl Companies, a family-owned and family-style–managed enterprise, wrestles with as it grows larger. It needs to create management levels to help ensure accountability, which, as Spiegelman says, "can be threatening to people." His number one objective, Spiegelman explains, "is to make sure that people know that as long as we build structure and bring in outside talent, the culture is not sacrificed." Beryl's success depends on employee engagement, and if factors arise that create disengagement, employee dissatisfaction will rise and business results will suffer.[28]

Tom Draude, former Marine brigadier general and CEO of the U.S. Marine Corps Foundation, likes the "beer truck scenario" when considering who is next in the line of succession. It goes like this: If you are run over by a beer truck on the way to work, "Who is going to succeed you? Who have you groomed to take your place?" Grooming, says Draude, goes beyond identifying a successor; it also includes "involving the [individual] in what you are doing." This way, potential successors see close up what it takes to manage as well as to lead.[29]

One way of testing this assumption is to put yourself on the front lines, as Draude did when he was assistant battalion commander of the First Marine Division in Operation Desert Shield/Desert Storm. There was fear prior to the invasion of Kuwait in early 1991 that the Iraqis under the command of Saddam Hussein would use poisonous gas to fend off the attackers. Soliciting feedback from the Marines who would execute the plan gave frontline troops the opportunity to provide their ideas and senior officers the opportunity to modify the plans. (Fortunately, no chemical weapons were used.)

Part of a leader's development process is being a good communicator. "The folks you are privileged to lead need to hear you tell them what's going on, the good news and the bad news. They need to hear it from you," says Draude.[30] This lesson is something that experienced leaders understand well. It comes to them early in their careers as they learn how to work not only with colleagues but also with direct reports. Yet I have found that they sometimes forget to share these lessons when they become senior leaders responsible for the development of emerging leaders. They make the assumption that the up-and-comers already know how to lead. Such an assumption is sadly false and one that causes a degree of hardship that could be avoided if the more senior leader took the time to make things relevant to younger colleagues.

What Works

As one who both writes and teaches, I am acutely aware of the leadership knowledge base of emerging leaders. Yet leadership is not something one picks up solely from a book or in a classroom. What most leaders have yet to manage, through no fault of their own, is how to apply such knowledge in their jobs. That is, a good number of rising managers know how to manage the work; they may have a degree in business or have picked up the basics from on-the-job training or even in-house management courses. What is lacking is how to apply the practice of management to the art of leadership. Management is the discipline of making systems go; leadership is the art of getting people to make those systems go well.

So what can a leader do to help educate the next generation of leaders? Here are some tips I've gleaned from watching how the best-of-the-best leaders do it:

• **Observe how the new leader is doing with his or her team.** While it is important to make certain the work is getting done, you also want to ensure that it is being done the right way. That does not mean mistake free; it means that everyone on the team a young leader is managing knows his or her job.

• **Follow up with direct reports.** Part of observation will be to talk to direct reports. A shrewd leader will ask questions about the output, but also be checking for signs that the team is engaged—that is, that people know their roles and are getting along with one another. So often young leaders make their numbers, but drive their people to distraction in the process either by excessive meddling or with overbearing management that is disruptive.

• **Make time to teach.** Schedule time with the manager to talk about how things are going. You want to ask his or her opinion of how things are going first. So often young leaders are so wrapped up in their tasks that they become overwhelmed and fail to notice how their direct reports are doing. So this is a good time to have a chat about how a leader needs to make time to check for understanding with his or her team, as well as be available to listen to their concerns.

At Henry Ford Health System in Detroit, leadership development is an organized effort, with four academies each focused on a different constituency: new leaders, middle managers, senior executives, and physicians. This allows lessons to be directed to the immediate needs of attendees, as well as serves as preparation for leaders to assume greater levels of responsibility in the future. But, as CEO Nancy Schlichting explains, commitment to development is a personal choice. Sometimes she meets employees who say they want to move up, but are not willing to make changes in their personal life to accommodate management responsibilities. Such boundaries are limiting, as are self-imposed limitations. Risk is inherent in leadership; to move up, the organization needs people who are "willing to step out of their comfort zone and demonstrate that they can do hard things that really will help them [to be] good candidates for promotional opportunities."[31]

Leaders who are grooming the next generation of leaders need to respect those candidates, says Tammy Erickson, who has authored best-selling books on generational issues. That can be a problem for some in the baby boom generation who are not comfortable with Gen X, whom they feel "don't demonstrate commitment to the organization in ways that we recognize." Their trust in institutions is not the same as that of their elders. "They tend to keep their options open," says Erickson. Baby boomers interpret that "options open" attitude as bad faith, when, in reality, it is a sense of honesty. Gen Xers do indeed work hard, but Erickson has observed that boomers feel uncomfortable when their employees are less than blindly loyal or not "professing continuous devotion."[32]

Leadership Is a Personal Choice

Just as everyone is not cut out for management, not everyone is cut out to be a leader. Some managers may take to managing systems well, but do not engage well with others. It is something they consciously avoid, and as a result, they revert to behaviors that alternate between abrupt and brash to distant and distracted—neither of which is suited to engaging the attention of direct reports. Coaching can help, but only when the manager is intent on improving his or her approach. When this happens, it falls to senior leadership to put such managers in places where they can put their skills to best use, either individual or collectively in a team.

Grooming that next generation of leadership is part of what good leaders do. They work regularly to make leadership lessons relevant in ways that help the up-and-comers gain insights that will help them become more effective with others. Tom Draude says that in his 30-plus years in the Marine Corps, "I couldn't wait to get up in the morning. And I'd do it all again in a heartbeat because I was so extremely happy." Leaders need to feel purpose inside. One technique Draude taught others was the Sunday night test, asking, "Are you looking forward to Monday morning?" Aside from bad days and bad weeks, "Life" says Draude, "is too damned short to go through dreading Monday morning." If so, then a leader "has to do something else."[33]

One way of coping is to deal with the workplace stress that can cause leaders to overreact. Draude says, "I will never chew somebody out on a Friday afternoon"; since it used to happen to him and would worry him the entire weekend, he resolved never to do it to others. "I can never understand leaders who thought they were going to succeed by beating up on their employees," he says. "That's not leadership, it's tyranny." If you don't have happy employees, asks Draude, how can you expect them to do a good job? Leaders can also relieve stress by admitting mistakes. At the same time, they need to close the loop with learning and resolution. In other words, Draude explains, they must admit, "I screwed that one up and boy did I learn from it . . . [and] we're going to do better."[34]

Draude continues, "The sine qua non [of leadership] is that you gotta like people. If you don't like people, go to a cave"—or do something where you don't need to work with others. Part of the leadership proposition is enabling others. "If you like people and you want to help them achieve success, what a golden opportunity leadership provides."[35]

Develop the Next Generation of Purposeful Leaders: Survey Results

What Employees and Managers Say

Over 90 percent of those surveyed say that the best way for leaders to groom the next generation of managers is by:

- Identifying high-potential employees
- Offering professional development
- Providing coaching and mentoring

Just under 80 percent of those surveyed believe that leaders should encourage job rotations as a means of development.

What Leaders Must Do

Preparing the next generation to lead is an essential task of management. Identifying those who can lead is a first step, followed by opportunities to develop talent and skills, as well as to assume greater levels of responsibility. Emerging leaders benefit from development plans that they work on with their managers; these plans can provide a roadmap to acquiring the skills and experience necessary to assume greater responsibilities.

Action learning projects developed internally give emerging leaders the chance to grow their skills. Job rotations accomplish the same purpose. Professional development outside the organization is also good, particularly when leaders have the opportunity to meet fellow leaders from different organizations. Coaching is an essential management responsibility; employees need feedback. Mentors, particularly those high up in the organization, can provide an emerging leader with valuable perspectives that can be integrated into a leader's development process.

How to Develop the Next Generation of Leaders

Leadership Questions

- How much of my time do I spend coaching my employees?

- How can I take greater ownership over the development of my employees?

- How well have I encouraged my employees to manage their careers?

Leadership Directives

- Make it known that leadership development is a responsibility of every level of management.

- Challenge employees to own their careers and look for ways to grow their skills.

- Make it known that employees need to have a work plan—that is, a roadmap for developing their competencies.

- Enable employees to attend courses to improve their technical and managerial skills.

- Encourage professional development as a leader.

- Be open to executives taking leadership roles in nonprofit community organizations.

- Encourage job rotations. Allow employees to learn new skills that enable them to work cross-functionally.

- Make it known that you are open to employees who want to increase their levels of responsibility.

CHAPTER 7

STEEL YOUR OWN PURPOSE

> "The secret of success is constancy to purpose."
> —BENJAMIN DISRAELI, SPEECH, JUNE 24, 1872

"No man, I believe, ever had a great choice of difficulties, and less means to extricate himself." That statement was expressed by a man at the end of a long year in which he had lost 90 percent of his troops. Strategically and tactically, the army under his command seemed inept. There was a move afoot to remove him from command, and even worse, the populace was turning against him. "I think the game is pretty near up," he told his brothers.

The author of these sentiments was not some hapless, down-on-his-luck general. It was none other than George Washington, our first commander-in-chief. Tempting as it might have been to resign, Washington did what so many other great leaders facing adversity do: counterattack. As we know from historian David Hackett Fischer, General Washington attacked the Hessian garrison at Trenton, and three days later crossed the Delaware and established a foothold from which he was able to withstand a British counterattack.[1]

Washington certainly knew a great deal about purpose. It is what steeled him during his long years of service to our nation. But as we know from this story, Washington also suffered from doubt. All good leaders do from time to time. The challenge is what to do about it. There are three lessons that any leader in crisis can learn from Washington's example:

1. **Do not wallow in misery.** Washington may have confided to his brothers that he was facing doubts, but he did not share that feeling with his fellow officers. Good leaders are those who find ways to acknowledge shortcomings, but look for ways around them. They turn self-doubt into an impetus for action.

2. **Make changes.** Being thrown out of New York City and having to escape to Long Island, and then losing subsequent battles, were indications to George Washington that change was in order. Again, as Fischer tells us, Washington revamped his command structure, improved the supply infrastructure, and altered his leadership style.[2] Effective leaders know that when things are not working, you need to look first at yourself before you ask others to change. Explore what it might be about your leadership style that is ineffective. You may be too hands-on or too hands-off. You may be acting tactically rather than strategically. And always, it's good to seek advice from others.

3. **Go on the offensive.** A nor'easter was pummeling New Jersey with snow as Washington decided to attack Trenton. Surprise was his advantage. Acting in the face of adversity can be a wake-up call for a

team. Just when he may be thinking that all is lost, the leader rallies his troops to action by pushing them to do the unexpected.

While these three steps worked for Washington, they do not tell the entire story. The American Revolution lasted another six years and our nation was not fully established for another decade. So these moves are not guarantees of success. You need to be honest with yourself and your team about what you can do. Acknowledging limits is not an admission of failure; it's a realistic assessment of your predicament based on resources and capability.

Nurturing Purpose from Within

Going against the odds can work. After all, Washington's victories at Trenton did not win the war, but they did help persuade the French to enter the conflict, the Americans to stop defecting to the Tories, and the British to reconsider their position. So while battling the odds may not bring the desired end results, it can energize your team and produce a short-term gain that instills confidence. Then, looking back, as we do on the battle of Trenton, such victories can be recognized as critical turning points. But that can only happen if you muster the gumption to accept your situation, rally yourself and your team, and seek to make a difference.

For Washington, action was a priority, but for business leaders, action must be coupled with intention. Thus far in this book we have explored what leaders need to do to instill purpose in their organizations and in their teams. Now it is time to explore how leaders can instill purpose in their own lives—because only when a leader is convinced of his or her own purpose can he or she effectively lead others.

Making Thinking a Priority

Sound purpose begins with sound thinking—with taking time to think before we do. On NPR's *Fresh Air*, Dr. Lisa Sanders told interviewer Dave Davies that physicians are compensated more for doing something than for thinking about it. Dr. Sanders, who writes the "Diagnosis" column for the *New York Times*, was referencing the fact that she was able to earn more for removing an ingrown toenail than for diagnosing a more serious medical condition. This differential between diagnosis and procedure affects how physicians are compensated. Debate over the merits of this has simmered in the healthcare community for years.[3]

The dichotomy between thinking and doing also lies at the heart of how leaders are perceived. Leaders are measured in terms of results—that is, what they and their teams accomplish. This is well and good, but too often the pressure for results pushes decision makers to do *some*thing, and do it *fast*, before they take time to consider the consequences. Leaders need to take a step back and make thinking a priority.

Thinking in advance is something no one is against, of course, but too often the press of business challenges us to act first and think later. We can think of too many products, chiefly software programs, that were rushed to market before they were ready in order to meet deadlines—and as a result, bombed because they were riddled with flaws. Some of those flaws might have been worked out if more upfront time had been spent on thinking through problems rather than patching over them to meet a scheduled deadline.

Taking time to think is a discipline that every manager needs to implement and practice regularly. For me, thinking involves a combination of assessment, diagnosis, reflection, and prioritization.

- **Assess the situation.** Managers need to know what's happening as well as what is not happening. Consider a project and its process. Is it on time and on budget? If so, why or why not? Consider what you and your team need to do next. You need to know where you stand now before you can act.

- **Diagnose the problem.** Identify the situation and decide what to do. It is fine to deliberate, but be deliberate in your process; that is, take care, but make it known that you need to make a decision within a given time frame. Hold yourself and your team to the process.

- **Reflect on the consequences.** Consider what the diagnosis means. For example, a major problem may involve going back to square one. More often, you can make an adjustment and correct the problem, then consider the "what's next?" Reflection also involves gaining perspective on where you stand.

- **Prioritize your thinking.** Every manager, at least those I know, seems to have more on his or her plate than time to digest it. If you add thinking to that plate, there may be even less time. So what smart managers do is delegate more tasks and responsibilities, so that they have enough time to spend thinking. You can also include your staffers in the thinking process. Invite them to assess, diagnose, and reflect right along with you. Also, make it clear that you'd like them to challenge your thought processes. This will make for more robust discussion and, occasionally, better ideation.

Thinking through the issues is not the same as failing to make a decision because you are drowning in data. The former is a virtue; the latter is a time waster that leads to "analysis paralysis." Its roots lie in a manager's lack of security, combined with a pressure to produce.

Managers end up overwhelmed with data and stuck in stasis, which brings everything to a halt.

Even Henry Ford, who implemented and expanded upon Frederick Taylor's ideas on time management, recognized the value of thinking. Legend has it that an efficiency expert hired by Ford complained about a man who worked right down the hall from Ford but seemed to be doing nothing. The efficiency expert had caught the man with his feet propped on his desk. Ford advised the expert to leave the man alone, declaring that the man, Edward "Spider" Huff, had "an idea that once saved us millions of dollars." Huff was an electrician who developed the magneto for the Model T and also served as Ford's mechanic when he set the land speed record in January 1904, shortly after the inception of Ford Motor Company.[4]

Leaders achieve by doing, certainly, but that doing is facilitated by some good, old-fashioned think time.

Maintaining Your Equanimity

As much as leaders need to think and plan, sometimes they need to take a deep breath and let the situation play out before they become personally involved.

In a letter to his brother, poet John Keats spoke of his appreciation for Shakespeare's ability to write with "negative capability."[5] Experienced actors know "negative capability" well. That is, when you play an evil character, you don't play the villainy aspect; you play the character as he might seem to himself, often compartmentalized from the pain and suffering he might be causing. The same applies to playing a hero. You don't play the heroism; you play the human being. The lesson for leaders, in the words of Shakespeare, is "To thine own self be true."

If the term "negative capability" sounds academic, think of it as equanimity—the ability to remain calm, to stand apart and judge a situation for what it is, to be comfortable with uncertainty. That's easy to do in the abstract, but not so easy in the heat of the moment or during a crisis, which is precisely when a sense of equanimity is most important.

We need our leaders to have a sense of distance. Michael Useem, a bestselling author and professor at the Wharton School, writes in his book *Go Point* about how leaders of mountain-climbing expeditions are often not right up on the summit with the climbers. They are further down the mountain, using their physical distance to make judgment calls with a perspective sharpened by that distance. Literally, they can see the bigger picture, which is essential when a weather front moves in or a climber gets in trouble.[6]

Essential to equanimity is patience, which (as your mother reminded you) is a virtue, and it's one that many people in power lack. The purpose of authority is to act, and so the concept of sitting back and watching is hard, very hard, to do. Consider it like watching your child play a sport. You don't experience the high of competition, but you experience the defeats, simply because you cannot do anything about them. Leaders need to cultivate patience before they can act. Here's how to cultivate your own sense of equanimity:

1. **Know the situation.** Good leaders are those who recognize context—that is, how a customer or a competitor will respond to an adverse situation. More important, they recognize the capabilities of their own people, what they can handle and what is beyond them. In addition, they know how to push their people the right way, to get

them to accept greater levels of responsibility as a means of addressing a tough situation.

2. **Let the dice roll.** Decisions have consequences. If a new project is not launching on schedule, or a new hire is not working up to speed, it may be better to wait and see what transpires. In this regard, leaders can learn from experienced negotiators who let the other side commit before they do. This takes skill, but also requires a belief in one's own abilities to figure things out.

3. **Take the long view.** Experience comes to the fore here. Emerging leaders might be tempted to exert their own influence rather than letting a situation unfold. But when you do that first, you prevent your team from learning. Better to advise your team to take action, and let them determine what happens next.

Equanimity is to be praised, but as with all things, too much of it is not good, either. Too much "apartness" can come across as disengagement, which will be perceived as not caring. That is fatal to a leader's credibility. Instead, there are times when a leader needs to jump in feetfirst and exert command. For example, some executives are superb "firefighters." When trouble strikes, they are ready to hop a flight to address the problem, be it to resolve a production glitch in a factory or meet face-to-face with a disgruntled customer. Also, they are willing to confront people on their own team who are not responding to direction or failing to hold themselves to the values of the culture.

Make the Most of Your Reflection Time

Too much action undermines a team's ability to function independently, but too little results in chaos. That is why the sense of equanimity, or balance, is so critical to leadership. In short, sometimes you breathe easily and lead, other times you do the heavy lifting.

The higher you rise in an organization, the greater the demands on your time. In my conversations with senior executives, one thing I have learned that they crave (nearly as much as access to the corporate jet) is time—time to do what they want and think they need to do, to think about what is happening and get perspective on the situation so they can act knowledgeably rather than reactively. Reflection is essential.

Such executives might take a page from a leader in the private sector who annually took a week or so off from the corporate scene to read, reflect, and regroup: Bill Gates. For years, while CEO of Microsoft, he spent time in a remote cabin in the Pacific Northwest, where he was accessible in an emergency but apart from the day-to-day flow of business. It is said that the origins of the Bill and Melinda Gates Foundation—the philanthropic project Gates created with his wife—took shape on one such retreat.[7]

For all those executives who protest that they do not have time, I challenge them: They are kidding themselves. They are perceiving reflection as a passive process. On the contrary, it can be an active and engaged form of self-dialogue, as well as one conducted with others. Here are some ways to reflect:

• **Do it in real time.** One of the most dramatic examples of reflecting in real time is the behavior of Colonel Hal Moore during the Battle of the Ia Drang Valley in Vietnam in 1965. Moore and his men helicoptered into a landing zone that turned out to be surrounded by more than 3,000 North Vietnamese. A 36-hour firefight ensued, and throughout the long battle, Moore was observed withdrawing from the action. During these periods, as related in the book

Hope Is Not a Method by Gordon R. Sullivan and Michael V. Harper, he was asking himself three questions: What is happening, what is not happening, and what can I do to influence the action?[8] Those are powerful questions any executive can use in real time to get a fix on issues and problems and determine how to respond to those problems.[9]

- **Insist on it.** Crises will come and the need to confront them will arise, but very often a savvy leader will have time to carve out time to ponder the issues. President John F. Kennedy did this masterfully during the Cuban Missile Crisis; during the 13-day affair, he was in frequent consultation with his aides, as well as receiving briefing reports from civilian and military leaders. Kennedy had time to think through his options, and since the world did not "go nuclear," it seems that Kennedy made the right choices. So even when things seem hectic, find time to gather your thoughts and think through your options. Make time, as Kennedy did, to listen to different points of view.

- **Value it.** Skip LeFauve, the former president of Saturn Corporation and a longtime General Motors executive, once told me that if you wanted time to reflect, you put it on your calendar. Skip was big on using his reflection time to have a dialogue with a trusted colleague, often about people issues. It is important to gain perspective on the moment as well as the situation; doing this with another person makes the process more practical, and within a management culture, more doable.[10]

Leaders are besieged with requests for their time and attention, not just sometimes but nearly all of the time. Nonetheless, leaders owe it to themselves to hold something in reserve, even if it is only for themselves. As a leader, you need to pull away from the fray and spend some time on *you*, apart from personal time for friends and family. This is personal executive time during which you think about what you are doing, why you are doing it, and what the consequences of your actions might be.

Reflection is a critical leadership behavior. You don't have to wait until the sun is shining and the birds are singing to reflect. Nor do you need to hole up at your favorite fishing spot. The important thing is to do it. Make the most of reflection, and it will pay itself back in terms of higher-quality decisions, as well as a more deliberative leadership practice. How much time you reflect is up to you.

Avoid Becoming a Caricature of Yourself

Reflection is a useful tool for gaining perspective on yourself, as well as for keeping an eye on your own foibles. "As one gets older, one becomes a caricature of his own self," postulates surgeon-biographer Dr. Gerald Imber, in an interview on NPR's *Fresh Air*.[11] Veteran leaders would do well to ponder Imber's assertion because often the traits that make a leader effective in the beginning can erode his or her ability to lead over time.

Caricature certainly applies to Dr. William Halsted, whom Dr. Imber (a plastic surgeon by trade) profiled in his biography *Genius on the Edge: The Bizarre Double Life of Dr. William Stewart Halsted*. Halsted was a pioneering nineteenth-century surgeon who revolutionized surgical care, but he had some quirks that were hard to overlook. As Dr. Imber recounts, Halsted was "obsessive and rigid . . . a perfectionist in certain portions of his life [but also] totally negligent and totally forgetful. . . . For example, he could leave a patient in a hospital bed for weeks on end and forget to operate on them. . . . No one would ever remind him because they didn't want to incur his wrath."[12] Halsted also became addicted to cocaine and later morphine.

Such dichotomies can plague business leaders, too. A leader who is aggressive and bold on the way up may seem overbearing when working as a functional chief. His desire to be the prime instigator of initiatives may strike direct reports as micromanaging. Likewise, a leader who prides herself on leading through consensus will be perceived as a good team player. However, in a more senior role, that same executive may seem overly cautious and unable to make key decisions. Thus, you become a caricature, from a leadership perspective, when your quirks become amplified to the detriment of your good qualities.

We can draw an analogy, then, between entrepreneurship and leadership. The skills it takes to build a business—vision, initiative, and drive—are not the same skills as required to manage that business, which generally are alignment, execution, and discipline. Likewise, a leader on the way up must at first rely on his own skill set to make a name for himself, but sooner or later he needs to learn to delegate to others—otherwise he will stall out. While many senior leaders learn that lesson early on in their careers, sometimes, especially if they have remained at the top, they lose touch and revert to character—or more cruelly, to caricature. Here are some suggestions to keeping yourself focused and engaged:

• **Rethink what you do.** Consider this exercise. Take a clean sheet of paper and write down your roles and responsibilities. When you have itemized your tasks, reduce what you do to one or two key responsibilities. For a CFO, this might be arranging to secure financing for the firm. For a marketing chief, it might be positioning products for success. Then, look at your tasks and see what you might off-load to others so that you can have more time to focus strategically on your key responsibility.

- **Take a sabbatical.** As much as those in the corporate world snicker at professors who take leave with pay for six months or a year to pursue research or something new and different, there is good reason for taking a break: It is invigorating. Few executives can afford this kind of time away, but there are ways to create sabbatical-like activities, such as volunteer efforts, teaching programs, or even networking away from your firm that will enable you to adopt a fresh perspective.

- **Look for new challenges.** What else do you want to do? For some senior leaders, a promotion to the top job is a goal. For others, it might be to spend more time as a mentor to up-and-coming managers. For still others, it might mean looking to do something else outside the company—for example, working for another company or starting your own business.

There can be a plus side to being a well-defined character, however: You become known for what you are and what you can do. That is, if you are a hard charger or a deliberative decision maker, your direct reports know how to approach you. Your caricature becomes a form of consistency. You become known for it, and that is not altogether a negative.

Leaders need not abandon the traits that allowed them to succeed. The challenge becomes finding ways to channel that energy in new and direct ways, so that you lead more appropriately and effectively. Look for opportunities to delegate decision making and reward emerging leaders with more responsibilities. At the same time, these executives will be called upon to make the tough decisions necessary to run the business. That is leadership. Lead through others when possible, but lead decisively when the future is at stake.

Finding Light Along a Dark Path

Out of the night that covers me,
Black as the Pit from pole to pole,
I thank whatever gods may be
For my unconquerable soul.

—WILLIAM ERNEST HENLEY, "INVICTUS," 1875

The man who wrote those lines had every right to be feeling melancholic: His foot was tubercular and had been amputated. But William Ernest Henley did not succumb to his dark thoughts; he kept his mind sharp and in fact survived for another 26 years.

Anyone who is facing tough times might find Henley's words comforting. One man, in particular, found them to be of great solace. Nelson Mandela memorized the poem during his 27-year imprisonment on Robben Island off the coast of Cape Town, South Africa.[13] The sentiment expressed in this poem may strike some as old-fashioned, even corny; after all, Henley was a product of Victorian England, a society that embraced the concept of a stiff upper lip in the face of adversity. As much as we might chide that spirit today, there is great merit in remaining stout when times are tough. More important, this poem, like all words of inspiration, challenges us to look within ourselves for strength.

This excerpt above is just a portion of the whole poem, but the operative theme is life's journey. How we progress through it is our own responsibility, and so it might be worthwhile to consider ways we can exert authority over our own destiny. Here are some suggestions for doing so:

- **Size up your situation.** Know where you stand; but rather than focusing on the negatives, consider how fortunate you are. Think about your accomplishments as well as how much other people value your experience. Then, focus on the tough things, the challenges that you are facing now.

- **Fix your eyes on your goal.** What do you want to do differently? This may be an easy question, but it has profound implications. If you need to find a new career, then you may require more schooling, either formally (university) or informally (being mentored). Be clear about your goals. Also, be realistic about what you can achieve in a given time frame. Consider what you need to do and by what time.

- **Take the first step.** Having a goal is good; the challenge is to act on it. Sometimes we are intimidated by goals and overwhelmed by the process. Look for a pathway to your goal and tackle it one step at a time. For example, if you are looking for a new job, write your résumé, contact a recruiter, apply for positions, and use your social network for insights into potential employers. If you want to obtain your MBA, work on your application. If you want to build a business, seek venture capital. Start small and build from there.

- **Be prepared to trip.** If your goal is lofty (and frankly, it should be), then don't worry if you stumble and fall. There's no shame in stumbling. The challenge arises in what you do next. So take stock of yourself. Consider what went wrong. Perhaps you are not qualified for the position you want or the company is not hiring now. Think about what you do next. Readjusting your goal is an option, but so is continuing on your chosen path, this time with more knowledge and a better plan of action.

• **Keep moving.** Momentum is essential to fighting adversity. You need to continue to think about, as well as act on, the next steps. Thinking as it relates to individual action planning is a positive. Acting as it relates to doing something—applying, interviewing, and being recruited—is essential to progressing along your journey.

There will be dark moments—times when nothing will seem as if it is going your way. You will be plagued by doubts about yourself and your plan, but take heart. Here are the final lines of Henley's poem:

> It matters not how strait the gate,
> How charged with punishments the scroll.
> I am the master of my fate:
> I am the captain of my soul.

Steel Your Own Purpose: Survey Results

What Employees and Managers Say

Over 90 percent of those surveyed believe that leaders can best instill ownership and principles of accountability in employees by:

- Matching actions to words
- Holding individuals accountable
- Including accountability as a core value

Nearly three-quarters of those surveyed believe that leaders should teach principles of accountability. Sixty percent say that linking executive bonus compensation to results is important.

What Leaders Must Do

Accountability lies at the heart of leadership. One of the ways that leaders can ensure that they hold themselves accountable is to think about the consequences of their behavior. Employees are watching to see how leaders behave. When leaders act for the benefit of others, employees notice. If they put themselves first, employees notice that, too. The concept of teaching others accountability must be grounded in practicing it. That is why the concept of linking executive compensation to results resonates. If the organization succeeds, its leaders deserve rewards; if it does not, then no rewards should be forthcoming. Accountability matters.

How to Steel Yourself with Purpose

Leadership Questions

- From whom and from where do I draw inspiration?

- What am I doing to ensure that I make time to think before I act?

- How well am I reflecting on my purpose and how it affects my team?

Leadership Directives

- Embrace doubt as a means of discovering more about your motives as well as your capabilities. You can use doubt to gain perspective; put your doubts into the form of questions: Why do I want to focus on this task? How will what I am doing now help me to lead others? Why am I not satisfied with results so far? What should I do about it?

- Think of the people you admire who live purposeful lives. Consider what gives them their sense of direction. Think of how such purpose can help you become more purposeful, that is, more focused on what you want to accomplish as a leader.

- Keep a journal of what you are doing to make purpose a reality in your own life. Document specific things you do—for example, finding new ways to connect people in your team to the work they do.

- Develop a habit of reflecting on what you have accomplished: Think of what you have done well and what you could do better.

- Find ways to draw inspiration from those who set examples that you would like to emulate.

8 LESSONS FOR DRIVING PURPOSE THROUGHOUT THE ORGANIZATION

> "Have a bias toward action—let's see something happen right now. You can break that big plan into small steps and take the first step right away."
>
> —**INDIRA GANDHI, FORMER PRIME MINISTER OF INDIA**

P utting purpose to work for the organization is the challenge every leader faces. The lessons drawn from the experts interviewed for this book and the stories told here provide a firm foundation for how leaders can use purpose to achieve intended results. To make the lessons more accessible, I have developed a blueprint for leaders who wish for more explicit insights into how to drive purpose and how to turn it into a strategic advantage for their organization.

This section is your guide for using purpose to the best advantage in your organization. While the eight lessons presented here are based on real-life practice, you need to adapt them to your own organization. By doing this, you demonstrate not only a commitment to instilling purpose but also drive the creativity that is necessary to compete in today's rapidly evolving world.

Each lesson begins with a story and includes suggestions for driving purpose in ways that touch employees directly. The subsequent Action Steps are derived from what survey respondents (managers and employees) have revealed are important to them.

Lesson 1: Instill Purpose Throughout the Organization

Purpose resides in the heart of the organization. It is up to the leader to demonstrate it through behaviors and actions.

●　●　●　●　●　●　●

Men and women who get us to follow them are often those who, in the words of Abraham Lincoln, appeal to the "better angels of our nature."[1] When we feel that the leader is well intentioned and wants what is good for us and our organization, we naturally want to follow. If that leader can cause us to feel that by following him or her we are better people for doing so, that is special, indeed. The history of civil rights teaches us this: People embraced Dr. Martin Luther King Jr. not only because he was smart, eloquent, and moving but also because by following him, they felt better about who they were.

To a much lesser degree, but in a very visceral way, rooting for our hometown sports team—be it the Yankees or Dodgers, Patriots or

Chargers, Celtics or Lakers—makes us feel good because we assume they are "one of us." (Of course, they are not, but we feel as if they are.) However, getting people to follow us because they feel as if we are "one of them" can be taken to extremes. Take the example of Huey P. Long, the governor of Louisiana in the 1930s. He rode the wave of populism all the way to the governor's mansion in Baton Rouge. Long, a charismatic speaker with charm and appeal, promised much and delivered better roads, hospitals, and schools. But to achieve his aims—and to stay in power—he used bribes and kickbacks to grease his way. At the time of his assassination, he was a virtual dictator with intentions for national office. Yes, people liked Huey because he was one of them, but the price was too high and the dream died with him.

Leaders who make people feel better about themselves are very powerful and can accomplish great things. In ancient Greece, Epaminondas rallied the yeoman class of Boeotia to fight against the hated Spartans and twice defeated them in battle, the second time destroying Sparta's ability to invade again. Epaminondas's appeal was directly tied to his ability to make the farmers feel good about taking up arms against the enemy that had brutalized them for so many years.[2] In business, people embrace Whole Foods because they like the selection of foods, natural and otherwise, but also because they feel good shopping in a place that treats its employees well and lives its creed of sustainability as much as possible.

Appealing to the better self can be an important aspect of leadership. While it may be hard to cultivate, per se, it can be developed in leaders' approach to work and its effect on others. Here are some ways:

- **Live it.** Leaders who inspire followership for a while may be good speakers and radiate charisma, but leaders who inspire followership over time are those who live their example daily. Contrast the vagabond collegiate coach who hopscotches from school to school in pursuit of more cash and more acclaim with the high school coach who stays at one school preparing his or her athletes to be better players, as well as better students and people. Those latter coaches live their example every day in the hours they invest in coaching, cajoling, challenging, and counseling the kids they teach. Every city can boast at least one or more such men and women. They live the example and it is real.

• **Show the impact.** We live in a skeptical society; people have options, even at work when they are on the payroll. Compliance is one thing; commitment is another. One way to nurture commitment is to show people how their products or services impact customers or clients. For a time, the Saturn Corporation, a division of General Motors, invited customers to visit their factory; it was a time for Saturn workers to meet Saturn owners. Not only was it a marketing event, it was a way for workers to see the fruits of their labors. And it made them feel good about what they did.

• **Recognize the outcomes.** When people achieve something, take notice of it. "Good news" e-mail blasts do not cut it. You need to show people that their work matters. For example, when a manager not only does his job but along the way also reduces turnover and grooms employees for advancement, honor him for it. Make it known how special this individual is. Turn this person into a master manager, whereby he can teach what he knows about people to others.

Rallying people to a cause greater than themselves enriches your leadership. Persuading people to follow you because they like how they feel about themselves cannot happen overnight, though; in fact, it may never happen. But if a leader can persuade people that they can achieve something for themselves, and feel good about doing so, then you have the power, together with the organization, to accomplish much good.[3]

Action Steps

- Demonstrate to employees how their work matters by bringing customers to the workplace; or allow employees to visit places where their products or services are being used by customers.

- Tell stories about how products and services are being used.

- Create a "Customer Day," when employees and customers can meet and mingle.

- Implement a merit system based on performance; allow employees input into how the system should operate.

- Follow through on what you promise.

- If you fall short on a commitment, do not pretend otherwise or hope that no one will notice. Be the first to acknowledge it; explain why it happened and tell what you will do to remedy the situation.

- Instill confidence throughout the organization. People want to believe in a leader who believes in them. Find ways to share that confidence with others.

- Find inspiration in the work.

Lesson 2: Enable Employees to Be Purposeful

Implementation of purpose depends on how well it resonates in the hearts of your employees.

● ● ● ● ● ● ●

Sometimes the best way to understand what makes an organization purposeful is to look at a dysfunctional one, such as that featured in the hit TV show *The Office*.[4]

"He doesn't get people" is how actor Steve Carell describes the character he plays on the show.[5] Michael Scott, the boss, is woefully and pitifully out of tune with the people he manages. He constantly crosses the line between professional and personal worlds, and as a result does the inappropriate things, people-wise. Scott criticizes when he should not, micromanages others constantly, and never takes responsibility for any consequences—it's always someone else's fault. The conceit of the show is that Scott believes he is a great manager, one who leads his people by example, when in reality he is a complete fool. Of course, it works as comedy, and is a large reason for the popularity of the series, both in the United States and in Britain, where it originated.

Another reason for the popularity of *The Office* is that everyone seems to have worked for or with a Michael Scott–type boss. That's funny, yes, but also terribly sad and truly indicative of the sorry state of management in our culture! Sometimes managers are like schoolteachers. We expect so much of them, but we fail to provide them with the education, training, and resources they need to succeed. Then, we hold them solely accountable for failing schools. Likewise, managers by and large do a good job of getting things done, but so often their people skills leave much to be desired; as a result, organizations underperform. As with underprepared teachers, we have underprepared managers.

Senior managers need to do a better job of preparing people to *lead* other people, not simply to manage. Again and again, the most successful companies, as judged by factors such as revenue, profit, recruitment, and retention, are those that emphasize leadership at every level. Leadership development should not be the sole purview of human resources; it needs to be the responsibility of the senior-most people. Yes, this is what General Electric does, but so do Google, Xerox, Whole Foods, American Express, and so many more. These companies have robust leadership development programs; but genuine leadership development does not occur in a program setting. It occurs on the job: manager to manager, colleague to colleague. So, how can you cultivate a culture of leadership one-on-one?

• **Start with people.** Leadership is all about people. The more you develop them, the better odds you have for success. The same goes for managing them. Management goes awry when it measures only performance as it relates to task rather than to others. Yes, a manager needs to get results, but she also must do it the right way— that is, with people, not in spite of them. When you hold people accountable for their behavior toward others, you demonstrate that people matter. It is not enough to make the numbers; you must also do it with respect for others and function with them in a cooperative and collaborative manner.

• **Challenge them.** Leaders prove their mettle by taking on challenges. Savvy managers take their high-potentials and put them in situations that stretch their abilities. This leadership model is borrowed from military training, but it applies to the corporate world when you give people stretch goals related to their jobs. Challenging people also means supporting them with advice and resources. Without such support, you set people up for failure, which is also a good way to alienate good people.

• **Debrief and reflect.** No job is complete without a review. Look at what went right as well as what went wrong. Often you learn more from mistakes than successes. Sometimes success happens in spite of itself, a function of a good team and good product producing good results. Failure, however, can occur with those same things in place, but with poor managerial decisions. Reflecting on the pluses and minuses is critical. Equally critical is understanding that failure is not grounds for dismissal.

Leadership is not a "nice to have," it is a "must have." If organizations are not developing people to lead, then their business propositions will not last over the long term. Your company may succeed for a while, but in time incompetent managers will triumph. They will drive the good people away, leaving only the incompetent. People want to work for bosses who treat them as contributors, not simply as doers. Employees will put up with management shortcomings for a while, but when something better comes along, they will be gone.

Steve Carell remembers something that the actor Ricky Gervais (who had created *The Office* in Britain and played the equivalent of Carell's character there) told him: "If you don't know Michael Scott, you are Michael Scott." Let that serve as a lesson to anyone of us in management. Be in tune with what's going on around you.[6,7]

Action Steps

- Employees want to know that their compensation is competitive with other organizations. Distribute industry survey data to confirm that your organization is competitive. If you choose not to do this, explain why not.

- Invite employees to suggest ways to improve levels of compensation or alternative forms of compensation in addition to salary. Bonuses may work for some organizations. For those that cannot offer them, consider ways of providing compensatory time for long hours and increasing personal days.

- Find ways to recognize employee achievements. Do it in ways that are meaningful to employees.

- Develop career roadmaps that will show employees a path to higher levels in the organization. Be explicit as to the education, skills, and development needed to achieve such levels.

- Encourage employees to develop career plans that are designed to grow their professional and leadership skills.

- Insist that employees develop work plans that describe the skills they must have to do their jobs now and in the future.

- Make it known that the success of the organization depends on promoting employees from within.

- Share stories of individuals who have risen through the ranks. Invite them to mentor others within their same functions.

Lesson 3: Use Customers to Teach Employees Purpose

Clarity of purpose enables employees to see what is expected of them. It falls to the leader to deliver clarity by helping employees understand what customers expect.

●　●　●　●　●　●　●

A colleague of mine was telling me about an assignment he was doing for one of his clients. It involved a series of in-depth phone interviews with the client's customers on business issues and challenges. I asked him how much involvement his client had in the phone calls. "They listen, but don't say anything," my friend replied. *That's not good*, I thought.

Although my colleague is adept at interviews and is doing great work, he really should not be doing this job. His client should be conducting the interviews as well as listening.

Performing customer surveys and staffing customer call centers via outsourcing may be fine, but when it comes to having meaningful interviews, or dialogues, with customers, the clients need to play a central role. It is only by actively engaging these customers in conversation that you learn what a customer really wants or, more important, expects and maybe even aspires to.

Getting to know your customer is a leadership priority because fulfilling customer needs is what you are in business to do. Value can be a product, a service, or a better way of doing things. For this reason, client dialogues are essential. Entrepreneurs know this well; they live and breathe the same air as their customers; but when organizations grow and develop, frequently distance from the customers grows, too.

That's why it's important to remain in touch when you can. Here are some suggestions:

- **Hold regular conversations.** Talk to your customers regularly. Not once a year, but once, twice, or three times a month, at least. Find out how their businesses are doing. As you close the conversation, find out how your product offering is doing. Answers can and will head off disputes and problems, and may give you greater insights into your customers' world.

- **Ask for feedback and advice.** Think you know all the answers? Of course not, but sometimes we act this way when we speak to our customers. We assume they use our offerings the way everyone else does. So listen to them. Ask them for feedback. Don't be afraid to find out what you could be doing better. Customer suggestions can lead to a new product line. Or make a simple courtesy call once every six months. Again, you won't know until you ask—and listen.

- **Create customer days.** If you can bring your child to work, why can't you bring a customer? After all, the customer is the one paying the bills. You can call it "Customer Appreciation Day," but that's a misnomer. It's really "Customer Chat Day," when you introduce your customers to people behind the scenes. Putting your support staff together with customers will lead to greater understanding and more mutual engagement.

Don't forget: Most often, "customers" are not just the people opening their wallets. They may, in fact, also work for the same organization as you do. Treat them with the same courtesy and deference as you do paying customers. Those can be trying situations, sure. Internal customers can be tougher than nails, meaner than wolverines, and as inflexible as iron, but they are people just like you. If you break the ice with a warm handshake, or extend an olive branch to a "hostile party," you may make some headway. After all, there can be no value in not communicating, but plenty of value derived from talking and listening.

Action Steps

- Communicate the vision throughout the organization. Insist that every leader develop a vision for his or her function that complements the vision, mission, and values of the organization. This is one way to create a shared vision.

- Set clear expectations. Challenge leaders at every level to link performance to the organizational mission. Insist that personal behaviors complement the values of the organization.

- Engage in strategic planning. Challenge direct reports to develop plans that underscore the strategic intent.

- Provide opportunities to study business trends. Make certain people in the organization have access to industry publications and resources.

- Enable employees to attend conferences relevant to their discipline (e.g., accounting, marketing, human resources).

- Encourage employees to attend industry functions such as seminars and trade shows.

- Find ways to learn more about business trends from key vendors.

- Invite leaders of your company to present to the board of directors. When appropriate, invite them to receptions and dinners with members of the board.

Lesson 4: Manage for Purposeful Innovation

The reason purpose matters is that it lays the foundation for the leader to allow others to think, create, and innovate.

● ● ● ● ● ● ●

It may not be just CEOs who lie awake nights worrying. It could also be shareholders of any company or anyone else who has need of products or services in the healthcare, technology, oil and gas, government, utilities, or telecommunication sectors. What's their worry? The lack of qualified middle managers.

According to a study by Bersin & Associates of 750 business and 55 HR executives, there are three converging trends—economic growth, changing workplace demographics, and corporate spending constraints—that are negatively affecting businesses' ability to retain middle managers, as well as to recruit and train their replacements. Another study, by the Conference Board, of 769 CEOs in 40 countries revealed that "finding qualified managerial talent and managerial success had become the dominant people issues for American CEOs."[8]

These studies, among others, point out that this lack of managerial talent extends beyond demographics—that is, baby boomers are beginning to retire, but their replacements may not be readily available. One reason may be the perception among many younger persons that management is not a worthwhile pursuit. Image is one thing; quality of work is another. For technical workers and engineers, both of whom are in fields suffering managerial shortages, becoming a manager means giving up what you enjoy doing most—working on and solving technical problems. As a manager, the issues become more people based, and for many in these fields, solving these problems is less satisfying, especially if no management training or development is provided.

Therefore, the challenge for senior leaders in any organization, including those in human resources, is to find ways to elevate the practice of management by instilling it with a greater sense of purpose. One way is to fuse the concepts of leadership with those of management. Management governs the discipline of getting things done. Leadership covers how those things are done and by whom. You can manage without leading, but if you blend management skills with a focus on people, you can achieve higher levels of performance for the team and the company. Here are some suggestions:

• **Management starts with people.** Management is about getting results by putting the right people in the right places with the right resources. The second and third components are usually taken care of; it is the people quotient that often gets lost. Managers need to focus on people needs; if they do not like supervising others, then management is not for them. Yet for reasons of compensation and promotion, people get pushed into management when they would rather be doing "bench work"—that is, working in their own competencies. Organizations need to make it clear that management is not for everyone; it involves people, first and foremost. Put people first, or do not become a manager at all.

• **Management includes competency.** One of the toughest things for managers to do, especially those in engineering, healthcare, and design, is to sacrifice doing what they love doing most. For engineers, it is working on problems. For nurses, it is taking care of patients. For designers, it is creating new things. However, management need not mean total surrender of one's competency and passion. New approaches to job design can ensure that managers have time to pursue their passions as well as run their teams. Organizations need to teach managers how to derive joy and satisfaction by working with and through others. For example, engineering managers can be involved in creative work by providing direction as well as being available to problem-solve when needed. This makes management less administrative and more people and mind engaging.

- **Management embraces risk.** Management, by nature, involves developing plans, reaching milestones, and adhering to budgets. Those are linear steps that ensure that A follows B so that we get to C. However, success today often includes the ability to deal with or anticipate game-changing strategies and disruptive technologies that can wreak havoc with carefully wrought plans. That is why managers need to be taught to embrace risk as well as to look for it; that way, when unexpected things happen managers have the knowledge and permission to respond quickly. Risks need to be managed, of course, and that's where the tradition of management excels.

Elevating the managerial profession will not be easy; it requires adopting a new mindset. Just as companies break up policies and processes to become more creative, those same companies have to take a hard look at what goes into the practice of management. What worked a generation ago is not working now. Innovation demands letting go of the past in order to think about the future. The same may apply to managerial thinking. New emphases on people-development strategies that include coaching, leadership development, and on-the-job risk taking are essential to developing a new generation of management.

Josh Bersin, of Bersin & Associates, says, "It is no longer enough to simply work harder to recruit and manage people. Organizations must now work smarter and take a holistic and integrated approach to identify, source, recruit, and develop talent."[9] In other words, developing managers is not simply the purview of human resources; it must be a top priority for senior leaders and everyone who aspires to senior leadership. If not, management in the early twenty-first century may be more defined by *Dilbert* and *The Office* than by solid results reflected on the balance sheet.

Action Steps

- Challenge everyone to think creatively. Make it known that creativity is something in which any employee at any level can participate. Publicize ideas that employees contribute and reward those ideas that improve any one of the following: the workplace, policies and procedures, work processes, the work environment, sustainability goals, or the bottom line.

- Identify what it takes to innovate: a commitment from senior leaders, adequate resources to allow experimentation, a supportive work environment, an ample tool kit, and a sense of individual accountability.

- Provide employees with free time to create when they demonstrate the ability to devote themselves to projects that complement the organizational vision and mission.

- Create internal think tank–style incubators where colleagues from different disciplines can come together to exchange ideas. Arrange for brainstorming sessions.

- Reward employees for putting ideas into action by publicizing their achievements. Show how their initiative led to the implementation of an idea that made a positive contribution to employees, customers, or shareholders.

Lesson 5: Monitor Your Purpose by Watching the Reactions of Others

Purpose buttresses the backbone of an organization, giving leaders and employees the freedom to create, to take risks, and sometimes to fail. Such freedom is essential to nurturing a healthy organization that can stand the test of time.

●　　●　　●　　●　　●　　●　　●

A few years ago I had the opportunity to watch a video shoot at a client facility. The executives were acting in a comedy skit that would be shown at an annual meeting. They were having fun spoofing themselves, and the net result was a downright funny piece. I noticed the director, a veteran of the famed Chicago comedy troupe Second City, take time to get reaction shots from key members of the cast. Anyone who knows comedy knows that what is often funniest, particularly on film, is not the funny line but the reaction of other characters to that line. The look of surprise, pain, or shock makes the gag pay off—it is the punctuation. Buster Keaton was the master of the silent deadpan. Today, as host of Comedy Central's *The Daily Show*, Jon Stewart's reactions to the reports of the program's "senior analysts" underscore the humor of his fake TV news show, drawn from a large bag of practiced raised eyebrows, fawning looks, feigned pain, and twisted grimaces. It is funny.

There is a lesson in this for leaders—people not typically engaged in making people laugh for a living: Pay attention to how people react to what you do or say. Carl Bass, President of technology company Autodesk, Inc., said that when he became CEO, "My IQ jumped ten points and I became much funnier."[10] What Bass discovered is that proximity to power can have unintended effects on people. Something said in an offhand manner will be taken as an order, or something left unsaid may give people license to ignore it. The higher the rank, the more a leader's actions have ripple effects. For that reason, leaders need to pay attention to their behavior, especially toward people over whom they have authority. More specifically, you need to stretch your frame of observation so that it covers what's happening now, as well as what may happen later. Here are some suggestions:

• **Watch what you say.** Words do matter. Be clear, coherent, and consistent, as well as frequent. Those are obvious lessons. Also, pay attention to how people react when you speak. Are they shocked? Bored? Confused? Do a check with people in the room to make certain you are understood. For important matters, follow up regularly to see that people are doing what you have asked them to do. Note: Ease up on the profanity when you are with subordinates. Yes, it is rampant in certain fields—market traders, entertainment, sports, and the military. But keep in mind that rough language can be offensive to people who are not inured to the culture.

• **Watch what you do.** Actions speak louder than words. For example, when the person in charge appears annoyed or irritated, people pay attention. The boss's displeasure can cause people to squirm or sink in their seats. Sometimes the stern look is necessary; it helps get people focused. On the other hand, there are times when the boss may be thinking about something else and as a result look frustrated when he is not. In medieval times, such looks could send a man to the chopping block; today they may send teams off on tangents, trying to please a boss who is not displeased in the least. Good advice for senior leaders is to get in the habit of relaxing the facial muscles.

- **Watch for what does not occur.** Bosses get pushed and pulled in multiple directions. It takes discipline to remember what you said—or didn't say. To ensure you stay on track, make notes of key decisions. Put notes into your planning schedule so you can be certain to follow up with people at key milestones. Also, make it known that your door is open. Insist on being in the loop, but not part of the loop. That is, you want information, but you don't want to be doing the work of the team.

Here's a note of caution. When you are the top dog, everyone is trying to curry favor with you. Beware of the person who brings you nothing but good news about himself and nothing but bad news about others. At the very least, that type is a suck-up; at worst, he is measuring your office and sitting in your chair when you are not around. He wants your job and is willing to treat others shamefully to get what he wants. Most leaders are adept at rooting out these "ferret types," but not always. As a result, the organization is poorer for their plotting and backstabbing.

Sooner or later all leaders have their twilight. Dwight Eisenhower is reputed to have quipped that leaving the presidency hurt his golf game: "A lot more people beat me now." That's a lesson in humility that every leader needs to keep front and center. Sometimes the legacy of leadership is less about individual actions than about collective actions, starting with the development of others to take the lead. That is a long-term reaction to what you do in the here and now, and so it is important to always lead with eyes and ears wide open.[11]

Action Steps

- Provide clear guideline for strategic direction. Make certain that employees know how their job complements the vision and mission of the organization.

- Challenge employees to think outside the box by giving them time to work on projects that they feel passionate about. Enable them to take risks with their ideas. Provide access to senior management when these ideas are ready for project initiation.

- Create internal think tank–style incubators by allowing employees time to work on projects about which they feel strongly.

- Establish "energy rooms" complete with smart technologies that enable people to work collaboratively.

- Provide senior-level champions for employee-developed projects. Such sponsorship will ensure that employees have the resources to implement their ideas.

- Recognize employees for taking risks that complement the vision and mission of the organization. If possible, reward them with bonuses or merit pay. Consider them for promotion to more senior levels of management.

- Recognize people who overcame job challenges. Tell stories of their achievements and publicize them throughout the organization. Invite them to share their stories with employees in different functions.

Lesson 6: Why We Need Purposeful Leaders at Every Level

When purpose is clear, it provides something upon which to build for the future. Such a future depends on harnessing the talents of employees and developing them to lead into the future.

● ● ● ● ● ● ●

In too many organizations, frontline managers are viewed as doers not deciders, implementers not contributors, and compliers not creators. If these precepts seem arcane, more in keeping with nineteenth-century management principles than twenty-first-century ways of managing, it is because they are, according to a recent study by McKinsey & Company. Unfortunately, this study found that these ideas are still au courant in today's world of frontline management, particularly in distributed management locations—for example, retail, transportation, and real estate. McKinsey concludes that such practices are making organizations "less productive, less agile, and less profitable."[12]

Most corporations operate on principles of hierarchy. That is good for ensuring the development and execution of strategy, but it falls flat, as the McKinsey study and others like it have found, when it comes to being responsive to change and responsible for people. One highlight of the study noted that managers were spending more time on transaction than transformation—that is, more on administration than people. In contrast, "at best-practice companies, frontline managers allocated 60 to 70 percent of their time to the floor, much of it in high-quality individual coaching." Additionally, such managers had more opportunities to make decisions and "act on opportunities."[13]

If I were a manager, I would use this information as my entrée to advocate for more autonomy, or what we might call "leading from the middle." Here are some ways to put your ideas into action:

• **Develop a plan of action.** Consider how you can be more effective in your job by making decisions that allow your department to be more responsive to customer needs and more accountable to corporate directives. In other words, look for things you can do to delegate tasks so you can focus on thinking more strategically for your team.

• **Become a person of influence.** Organizations operate on influence; those with influence get things done. Titles facilitate influence, of course, but truly influential employees are those who lead by their example. They are proactive; they think ahead. More important, they get things done on time and on budget. In short, they earn their stripes by following through.

• **Act more like a boss.** Supervisors should supervise the work, not do it. Avoid getting sucked into "feed the monster" tasks that satisfy immediate needs but only waste time. You can do this by thinking how you can effect positive change in ways that optimize value. This can take the form of optimizing operations, retraining employees, reducing costs, and spending more time with customers.

• **Be prepared for setbacks.** There used to be a saying in Hollywood that for every person who could say yes to your project, there were 50 who could and would say no! Those pushing from the middle need to steel themselves to push back. It will come not just from bosses, but from colleagues as well. Perseverance is essential to driving initiatives upward through an organization.

• **Believe in yourself.** Fortunate will be the manager who sells an idea upward the first time. Often it will take many tries to get your good ideas heard, as well as acted upon. During that time, continue to refine your idea. Listen to feedback. Most of all, don't lose faith in yourself. If your idea is rejected, find out why. Timing may be the reason. Put it away and plunge yourself into another project. A new day, or a new boss, may create new opportunities for you. Through it all, never stop believing in your ability to effect positive change.

Empowering managers to focus on people and make more decisions will be a challenge, but it is exactly what twenty-first-century managers need to do. Sharp administration is vital to efficiency, but managers can automate and delegate those skills so they have time to spend with their people to help problem-solve as well as think creatively about how to do things better. At the same time, there will be times when frontline managers will have to pitch in and help get the work done, either doing this themselves or finding extra folks to help out.

Focusing on the human equation of management pays off. Managers who have a degree of self-determination can do what it takes to improve their function, be it sales, manufacturing, or healthcare. Improving productivity is an imperative, especially in challenging times. Those who can lead from the middle, and are accorded the right to do so (as McKinsey advocates), will outperform their counterparts in more hidebound positions.

Action Steps

- Look at succession planning as succession development. Make it known that succession development is a partnership for organizational growth.

- Identify high-potential employees on a regular basis. Create a system by which employees who have the ability as well as the desire to move up are recognized. Provide them with mentors who can help them manage their careers.

- Offer cross-functional training so that employees can broaden their skills.

- Encourage job rotations so that employees have the opportunity to learn new things about the business.

- Present professional development opportunities. These can take the form of participation in in-house leadership and management programs or executive education courses. The former offer employees the opportunity to learn from senior leaders and bond with peers, while the latter offer a chance to learn new skills from executives in a variety of different fields.

- Provide coaching for high-potential employees. Assess their leadership capabilities and styles. Offer them the opportunity to work with an executive coach who can help them achieve their leadership potential.

Lesson 7: Leaders Need to Look Purposeful

While leaders nurture purpose in others, they must also take care to nurture their own sense of purpose so they have the confidence to lead and the strength to be accountable for their actions.

● ● ● ● ● ● ●

Does it matter what a leader looks like? According to a study by Tufts University researcher Nalini Ambady, reported in *The Economist*, people can judge a CEO's "competence, dominance, likeability, facial maturity . . . and trustworthiness" merely by his or her looks.[14]

Taken at face value (pun intended), this study makes for good reading in a lighthearted way. The evaluators were students and all the leaders studied were older white males. But the topic of looks is important to leaders. Is there something such as "the look of a leader"? Can we judge a leader by his or her bearing? How the person enters and exits a room? Of course we can. Leadership is an act, absolutely.

No one demonstrated that better than our first president, George Washington. He knew that as the first commander-in-chief, he had to look the part; he acted as a leader right down to his well-tailored uniforms, white horse, and white carriage. But he did more than work on his looks; he also worked on his presence, both figuratively and literally. He made himself available to his soldiers and his constituents, even long after he had retired to Mount Vernon.

So how can leaders work on their appearances? Here are some tips:

- **Look the best you can.** This is the easy part. Invite a trusted friend to evaluate your wardrobe. Women are at least 100 times (make that 1,000 times) better at this than men. If you are a senior leader, dress the part. It may require that you invest in some nicer, sharper suits, but it also means you want to invest in some good grooming, too. Wear your hair in a way that makes you look distinguished and trustworthy.

- **Focus on your expressions.** Relax. You don't have to look like the Great Sphinx or Winston Churchill. In fact, if you do, you will probably scare people and drive them away. So often we get absorbed in our own doings (and musings) that we forget how we look to others. Stern looks may be a sign of concentration, but on senior leaders they can frighten. Take a moment to relax your facial muscles; do it regularly. Then, if you have to turn up the heat, your looks will take on added magnitude and effect. People will pay attention.

•   **Be present.** Ronald Reagan allegedly once said that he was the only president who knew what he looked like from different angles. That is, having been a film actor, he was conscious of how he appeared in a variety of situations. Use that tidbit as you mingle with your people. Stop to talk and mostly listen. Engage in conversation. Imagine if someone took a picture of you. How would you like to look: stiff and uneasy, or relaxed and comfortable?

Looks do matter, but as anyone who works for an empty suit—one who looks good but ain't got what it takes to lead—knows: Character determines leadership. Example flows from character, so even if you look the part—clothes, hair, bearing, and attitude—you must back it up with actions. What you do for others, the team, and the organization matters more than how you look in the mirror.

Looks do matter, but character counts more. A manifestation of character in the workplace is accountability.

Action Steps

•   Take time to ensure that you "look the part" of a leader. Dress smartly but not extravagantly.

•   Remind yourself to focus your attention on people. As you do, relax your facial muscles. (Avoid using your smartphone when in conversation with others.)

•   Match actions to words. Do what you say you will do. Insist that direct reports do the same.

- Make time to exercise. Not only does it improve appearance but it can also improve your outlook because you will be feeling more fit.

- Teach accountability by making it known that everyone is accountable for his or her actions. Make certain that everyone knows that accountability is a core value of the organization.

- Executives need to hold themselves more accountable for results. When they achieve, they will be rewarded. When they do not succeed, they will lose merit pay.

- Do not allow a culture of accountability to devolve into a cesspool of blame. When people do not succeed, find out why they failed. Mistakes in judgment can be used as teachable moments.

- Link bonus compensation to results. When the team achieves its goals, consider ways to reward them financially. If this is not possible, then offer other forms of compensation such as compensatory time off.

Lesson 8: Tell Your Own Purposeful Narrative

Purpose in an organization can often best be expressed through stories of employees. Such stories capture the heartbeat of an organization by highlighting examples of those who make a positive difference.

•　•　•　•　•　•　•

When the USSR launched the world's first man-made satellite, *Sputnik*, into space in October 1957, it came as a shock to many in government, as well as those in the private sector. No longer was the United States the dominant superpower; the USSR seemed its equal—and in space, its superior. Some critics felt that the United States had been too complacent and as a result had lost its ability to compete. One person sought to do something about it, with a publication of essays centered on the theme of "national purpose." He was Henry Luce, the influential head of the Time-Life publishing empire.

Born in China as the son of missionaries, Luce always believed that his publications should do more than relate the news: They should influence how people should react to the news. His biographer Alan Brinkley speculates that Luce's desire to influence was rooted in his past; missionaries seek change, not the status quo.[15] Objectivity was not a hallmark of a Luce publication, and so Luce's stance is not a model of journalism, but he is a good example of how to use media to rally the public to a common cause, and for that reason he is worth remembering.

"National Purpose" began as a collection of essays by the leading minds of the mid-twentieth century. Among the contributors were James Reston of the *New York Times*, Billy Graham, the evangelist, and 1960 presidential candidates Richard Nixon and John F. Kennedy. Although the contributors all had different messages, a common theme was that America needed to rediscover its purpose if it were to continue to be the world's beacon of freedom and democracy.

This was a theme that Luce himself had explored in the run-up to the Second World War, in an editorial entitled "The American Century," which was a paean to American values and the obligation that Americans had to preserve democracy throughout the world.[16] *Life* magazine, a hugely popular pictorial publication, echoed such themes in its wartime coverage. It also documented, but also celebrated, post-war prosperity with cheery stories about the joys of consumerism and domesticity.

What we can learn from Luce is that, when you have a vision you wish to communicate, you must find ways to do so by inviting others to contribute to the story in their own ways. While Luce was politically conservative, and came to loathe the policies of Franklin Roosevelt's New Deal, many on the staffs of his publications were ardent Democrats. His publications typically backed Republican candidates, but it did not always toe the party line. Civil rights was a cause in which Luce was out of step with many conservatives. From our perspective today, we might say that, as an Anglo child growing up in China, Luce experienced diversity firsthand. *Life* magazine, in particular, documented the lives of African Americans at a time when they were ignored by mainstream media.

So while Luce's style of biased journalism may not be worth emulating, his commitment to communicating *purpose as he saw it* through his publications is worth remembering. What leaders can absorb here is the message that purposeful messages succeed because they are articulated—not only by you but also by others who share your intentions. Propaganda, by contrast, is singular in tone; it is one message or set of messages repeated over and over again. Purposeful messaging conveys ideas and intention, but through multiple voices, each with its own point of view.

"We do have a conscious say in selecting the narrative we will use to make sense of the world," according to *New York Times* columnist David Brooks. "Individual responsibility is contained in the act of selecting and constantly revising the master narrative we tell about ourselves."[17] Brooks's explanation about choice of narrative can apply to leaders seeking ways to navigate the future. The relentless tide of uncertainty may tempt those in charge to adopt a pessimistic viewpoint, but leaders owe it to their followers to spread optimism. Without excluding reality, leaders need to inspire not simply hope, but also resilience. Storytelling can help in this effort.

Here are some suggestions for crafting your own story to make sense of adversity.[18]

Use Your Authentic Voice

"Don't make me sound scripted!" is a caution that many writers hear from senior leaders for whom they pen speeches. What executives want is to sound natural and spontaneous. Most of all, they want to appear authentic. Is this possible if they don't write their own material? Of course. Good speechwriters know how to capture the speech patterns and rhythms peculiar to a speaker, as well as craft their anecdotes and stories.

The message, of course, is critical; it should reflect the values and beliefs of the organization, as well as its current strategies and objectives. All effective leaders in public life come to rely on scripting, from their public pronouncements to their schedules. But scripting words is only part of the leadership act; scripting the schedule—allocating time to activities, events, and interactions—-is equally important. What good leaders learn to do is make the script or the schedule work for them. Reliance on these tools does not hinder you as much as it may free you to accomplish more in a day.

Keep It Real

Of course, leaders must know how to live to the schedule or the script and make it seem real. They must live it by imbuing it with their character, as well as their passion. No one was better at this than Ronald Reagan; as a former actor, he was accustomed to scripts and knew how to make the character he played come alive. As president, the character was himself, and few fit the public role better. Reagan, however, was an effective writer; he wrote many of his own speeches, as well as many of the weekly radio addresses he gave prior to becoming president. As an actor, he knew how to take direction, and for that he relied on his staff—sometimes at peril to his presidency (as in the case of the Iran-Contra affair, when some overzealous staffers took his intentions too far and began selling weapons illegally).

The challenge for you is to maintain the balance between script—what you want to do—and what your staff wants you to do. The easy answer is to "write your own script." Strong leaders do dictate what they will accomplish during their tenure by issuing the vision and its accompanying themes. It is up to you to choose fellow leaders and staffers who will help you accomplish those goals. Here are some suggestions:

- **Share the dream.** If you want people to follow your lead, you have to give them a reason. You want people to share your passion. In one-on-ones, leaders convey that commitment to those who work with them. It is up to you to make your voice heard and presence felt throughout the organization. Telling stories about the progress that people within the organization are making is one way to get things rolling. Such stories do two things: Recognize individuals and demonstrate that you know what is going on. Engaging the audience through communications is critical. It must be the foundation of the script or the schedule. How you make it happen relies on personality and presence.

- **Be mindful of time.** No one, of course, knows how long he or she will remain in a given job. You may plan to be there for the long haul, but events—transfers, promotions, or new opportunities—may arise. Therefore, you need to use your time wisely, consider it as a gift. The higher you move up the ladder, the more people will want your time. Hoarding it will not work; you need to share it. Savvy CEOs are masters at this; wherever they go, they can focus on an individual for a given moment, taking the time, however brief, to engage in conversation and, more important, listen to what is being said. For the employee, this can seem to make time stand still. Urgency is not always the answer. There will be occasions when you need to take time to let events unfold, situations to clarify, or simply to gain perspective. In this regard, time is your ally.

•   **Revise your script.** Life does not work according to plan. Be it a war or a natural disaster, an unforeseen competitor, or a collapsing market, nothing is certain except this: Plans will change. It is up to you to go with the flow and to address the crisis or the challenge, often on the go. It is then you show your mettle under fire. Former governor (now Senator) Joe Manchin of West Virginia demonstrated his ability to connect with the voters as well as the world during the Sago Mine disaster in January 2006, when 13 miners were trapped underground. The world did not learn their fate for more than a day and a half, even after the miners' families were given incorrect information that the miners were alive. Only one survived. Manchin was front and center during the whole rescue mission, deflecting unwarranted publicity from the families but serving as the public face of advocacy. Sadly, Manchin had to repeat the entire act again in April 2010, when an explosion at the Upper Big Branch mine killed 23 miners.

Keep the Heart

Scripting, even on the fly, is good discipline, but there is one thing you cannot overlook: the heart. Leaders need to speak from the heart always, even when they are working from a script. The passion and enthusiasm must radiate from the words and delivery. But there will be public moments when, like Joe Manchin, you have to stand up and address tragedy in a way that gives meaning to the moment, even when hearts are breaking. No one did this better than Rudy Giuliani when, as Mayor of New York City on September 11, 2001, he seemed omnipresent. He was the public face of the crisis, as well as the public face of mourning, most especially in helping the city bounce back from the heinous terrorist attacks.

Living by a script may not seem spontaneous, but it is the way most good leaders accomplish their agenda. It is fine to go "off script" for a time, but too much off time will derail the momentum required to execute priorities in a timely fashion. Your challenge is to make each moment count, to live it to the fullest so that the energy you exert moves the organization forward. In the form of enthusiasm, that energy can be contagious; this is what matters most because it is the employees who do the heavy lifting, not the higher-ups. What leaders must do is what author E. B. White advised, "[M]ake the work interesting and the discipline will take care of itself."[19] Most of us do not live by a script, but when we love our work and its challenges, we will do what is necessary to pull off the task at hand, often better than we thought possible.

Telling your story is a means to an end, a way for you to stay focused on the task ahead as well as to help others who are connected to the work. Stories are a means of communicating purpose. As such, they link what you do now to what you will accomplish in the future. The more you connect the present to the future, the more connected to the work people will feel. Stories are a wonderful way to be purposeful in a manner that others find pleasing as well as rewarding.

Action Steps

- Look for stories within your organization. Identify the people who are making a positive difference; you might consider them the "heroes" of your organization. These are the folks who enable your organization to succeed.

- Develop a set of key hero messages—that is, vignettes about what these employees have done and how it has benefited stakeholders, whether customers, vendors, shareholders, or the community.

- Shine a light on the heroes of your organization. Make a habit of acknowledging the work that they do.

- Invite heroes to speak to customers and employees. Consider them "goodwill ambassadors" for your organization.

- Continue to look for new heroes. Whenever good news occurs, look to publicize the employees who made it happen.

2010 LEADERSHIP SURVEY RESULTS

The following are the results of the 2010 leadership survey conducted for the American Management Association (AMA) by NFI Research. As evident from the results of this survey, businesspeople see timely recognition as a key component of how leaders can best demonstrate that they truly do put people first. Almost all (98%) respondents said that timely recognition is key.

In terms of leaders being able to make a big difference in comforting employees regarding the unknown, 97 percent of executives, managers, and employees responding noted that setting clear expectations is important. The vast majority (95%) of respondents agreed that rewarding employees for putting their ideas into action is the best way for leaders to stimulate innovation and creativity. An overwhelming number (94%) of respondents agreed that leaders should encourage employees to take risks and show them that risks are integral to success by rewarding them for taking such risks.

By holding individuals accountable, and matching actions to works, 97 percent of respondents agreed that these are the best ways for leaders to instill ownership and accountability. Almost all executives, managers, and employees (98%) agreed that by providing coaching and/or mentoring, as well as professional development, leaders will be able to groom the next generation of managers. Nearly all respondents (97%) said that leaders will instill purpose in the workplace by linking work to results.

Note: This survey included 205 members of the American Management Association. Respondents were as follows: 14 percent were CEO, president, CFO, and so on; 63 percent were VP, AVP, director, and so on; and 23 percent were employees (including consultants).

Survey Questions and Responses

1. Leaders can best demonstrate that they truly do put people first by:

   (a) Providing competitive compensation

Strongly Agree	34.3%
Somewhat Agree	41.4%
Neutral	13.6%
Somewhat Disagree	7.1%
Strongly Disagree	3.5%

   (b) Delivering intrinsic awards (comp time, bonuses, etc.)

Strongly Agree	43.9%
Somewhat Agree	41.8%
Neutral	11.3%
Somewhat Disagree	2.5%
Strongly Disagree	0.5%

   (c) Offering developmental opportunities

Strongly Agree	77.4%
Somewhat Agree	16.4%

Neutral	4.1%
Somewhat Disagree	1.6%
Strongly Disagree	0.5%

(d) Providing timely recognition

Strongly Agree	78.9%
Somewhat Agree	19.0%
Neutral	1.1%
Somewhat Disagree	1.1%
Strongly Disagree	0.0%

(e) Promoting from within

Strongly Agree	47.8%
Somewhat Agree	33.2%
Neutral	10.2%
Somewhat Disagree	2.9%
Strongly Disagree	1.0%

2. Leaders make the biggest difference in making people comfortable with the unknown by:

(a) Providing vision

Strongly Agree	68.4%
Somewhat Agree	27.0%
Neutral	3.1%
Somewhat Disagree	1.1%
Strongly Disagree	0.5%

(b) Setting clear expectations

Strongly Agree	83.3%
Somewhat Agree	13.5%
Neutral	1.6%
Somewhat Disagree	1.6%
Strongly Disagree	0.0%

(c) Engaging in planning

Strongly Agree	55.6%
Somewhat Agree	32.9%
Neutral	9.3%
Somewhat Disagree	1.6%
Strongly Disagree	0.5%

(d) Providing opportunities to study business trends

Strongly Agree	21.1%
Somewhat Agree	44.4%
Neutral	27.3%
Somewhat Disagree	4.6%
Strongly Disagree	2.5%

(e) Promoting employee dialogues with key stakeholders

Strongly Agree	35.2%
Somewhat Agree	46.1%
Neutral	13.5%
Somewhat Disagree	4.7%
Strongly Disagree	0.5%

3. Leaders can best stimulate innovation and creativity by:

(a) Identifying what it takes to innovate

Strongly Agree	36.0%
Somewhat Agree	38.2%
Neutral	18.1%
Somewhat Disagree	5.2%
Strongly Disagree	2.5%

(b) Creating internal think tank–style incubators

Strongly Agree	27.3%
Somewhat Agree	47.9%
Neutral	17.0%

Somewhat Disagree	5.2%
Strongly Disagree	2.5%

(c) Providing employees with free time to create

Strongly Agree	29.2%
Somewhat Agree	34.3%
Neutral	27.2%
Somewhat Disagree	5.7%
Strongly Disagree	3.6%

(d) Challenging everyone to think creatively

Strongly Agree	53.1%
Somewhat Agree	31.0%
Neutral	11.3%
Somewhat Disagree	3.6%
Strongly Disagree	1.1%

(e) Rewarding employees for putting ideas into action

Strongly Agree	66.8%
Somewhat Agree	22.0%
Neutral	3.9%
Somewhat Disagree	0.5%
Strongly Disagree	0.5%

4. Leaders can encourage employees to take risks and show them it is integral to success by:

(a) Challenging employees to think outside the box

Strongly Agree	54.4%
Somewhat Agree	32.6%
Neutral	10.4%
Somewhat Disagree	1.6%
Strongly Disagree	1.1%

(b) Creating internal think tank–style incubators

Strongly Agree	50.0%
Somewhat Agree	37.5%
Neutral	8.9%
Somewhat Disagree	3.1%
Strongly Disagree	0.5%

(c) Rewarding employees for taking risks

Strongly Agree	66.8%
Somewhat Agree	27.0%
Neutral	4.1%
Somewhat Disagree	2.1%
Strongly Disagree	0.0%

(d) Providing clear guideline of strategic direction

Strongly Agree	66.4%
Somewhat Agree	26.8%
Neutral	5.2%
Somewhat Disagree	1.6%
Strongly Disagree	0.0%

(e) Recognizing people who overcome job challenges

Strongly Agree	66.2%
Somewhat Agree	21.8%
Neutral	9.3%
Somewhat Disagree	2.1%
Strongly Disagree	0.5%

5. Leaders can best instill ownership and accountability in employees by:

(a) Teaching principles of accountability

Strongly Agree	37.8%
Somewhat Agree	36.8%

Neutral	17.1%
Somewhat Disagree	5.7%
Strongly Disagree	2.6%

(b) Linking executive bonus compensation to results

Strongly Agree	33.6%
Somewhat Agree	27.4%
Neutral	26.8%
Somewhat Disagree	6.4%
Strongly Disagree	5.8%

(c) Matching actions to words

Strongly Agree	74.5%
Somewhat Agree	22.4%
Neutral	2.6%
Somewhat Disagree	0.0%
Strongly Disagree	0.5%

(d) Holding individuals accountable

Strongly Agree	76.9%
Somewhat Agree	20.4%
Neutral	2.1%
Somewhat Disagree	0.5%
Strongly Disagree	0.0%

(e) Including accountability as a core value

Strongly Agree	69.3%
Somewhat Agree	22.9%
Neutral	5.2%
Somewhat Disagree	2.6%
Strongly Disagree	0.0%

6. The best way for leaders to groom the next generation of managers is by:

(a) Identifying high-potential employees

Strongly Agree	54.1%
Somewhat Agree	38.6%
Neutral	6.2%
Somewhat Disagree	0.5%
Strongly Disagree	0.5%

(b) Offering cross-functional training

Strongly Agree	61.1%
Somewhat Agree	30.0%
Neutral	7.7%
Somewhat Disagree	1.1%
Strongly Disagree	0.0%

(c) Encouraging job rotations

Strongly Agree	45.6%
Somewhat Agree	33.3%
Neutral	16.4%
Somewhat Disagree	4.6%
Strongly Disagree	0.0%

(d) Offering professional development

Strongly Agree	73.7%
Somewhat Agree	24.7%
Neutral	1.1%
Somewhat Disagree	0.0%
Strongly Disagree	0.5%

(e) Providing coaching and mentoring

Strongly Agree	85.0%
Somewhat Agree	12.9%
Neutral	2.1%

Somewhat Disagree	0.0%
Strongly Disagree	0.0%

7. Leaders will instill purpose in the workplace by:

(a) Communicating the vision

Strongly Agree	73.7%
Somewhat Agree	22.7%
Neutral	2.5%
Somewhat Disagree	0.5%
Strongly Disagree	0.5%

(b) Linking work to results

Strongly Agree	68.5%
Somewhat Agree	28.3%
Neutral	2.1%
Somewhat Disagree	0.5%
Strongly Disagree	0.5%

(c) Implementing merit pay system

Strongly Agree	26.6%
Somewhat Agree	41.1%
Neutral	26.1%
Somewhat Disagree	3.6%
Strongly Disagree	2.6%

(d) Showing how customers benefit from what employees do

Strongly Agree	59.0%
Somewhat Agree	35.9%
Neutral	4.1%
Somewhat Disagree	0.5%
Strongly Disagree	0.5%

(e) Doing what they promise

Strongly Agree	81.9%
Somewhat Agree	13.4%
Neutral	4.1%
Somewhat Disagree	0.5%
Strongly Disagree	0.0%

(f) Instilling confidence

Strongly Agree	71.6%
Somewhat Agree	21.6%
Neutral	6.2%
Somewhat Disagree	0.5%
Strongly Disagree	0.0%

NOTES

Chapter 1

1. Peter Cappelli, Harbir Singh, Jitendra Singh, and Michael Useem, *The India Way* (Boston: Harvard Business Press, 2010), p. 5.
2. Pat Williams, interview, August 6, 2010.
3. Michelle Rhee, interview, August 3, 2010.
4. Ibid.
5. George Reed, interview, September 28, 2010.
6. Viktor E. Frankl, *Man's Search for Meaning* (Boston: Beacon Press, 2006).
7. Martin Dewhurst, Matthew Guthridge, and Elizabeth Mohr, "Motivating People: Getting Beyond Money," *McKinsey Quarterly*, November 2009.
8. Ibid.
9. Nicholas Christakis and James Fowler, "Dynamic Spread of Happiness in a Large Social Network," *BMJ*, December 4, 2008, cited in Pam Belluck, "Strangers May Cheer You Up, Study Says," *New York Times*, December 4, 2008.
10. Jim Guest, interview, August 31, 2010.
11. Roger Webb, interview, August 14, 2010.
12. Paul Spiegelman, interview, August 31, 2010.
13. Dan Denison, interview, August 3, 2010.

14. See denisonconsulting.com/advantage/researchModel.aspx.

15. Denison, interview.

16. Nancy Schlichting, interview, September 8, 2010.

17. Ibid.

18. Spiegelman, interview.

19. Ibid.

20. Small Giants Community takes its name from Bo Burlingham's book, *Small Giants: Companies That Choose to Be Great Rather Than Big* (New York: Portfolio Books, 2005).

21. Guest, interview.

22. Ibid.

23. Tom Draude, interview, August 27, 2010.

24. Ibid.

25. Ibid.

26. Ibid.

27. Ibid.

Chapter 2

1. "Bind up your wounds" comes from the Gettysburg Address, delivered by Abraham Lincoln, November 1863.

2. John Carlin, *Playing the Enemy: Nelson Mandela and the Game That Made a Nation* (New York: Penguin, 2009), pp. 163–64. The meeting between Nelson Mandela and Francois Pienaar is dramatized in the movie *Invictus*, written by Anthony Peckham and directed by Clint Eastwood.

3. Marshall Goldsmith, interview, August 14, 2010.

4. Nancy Schlichting, interview, September 8, 2010.

5. Ibid.; information on Henry Ford Health System, henryford.com/content/ourpeople.

6. George Reed, interview, September 28, 2010.

7. Ibid.

8. Tom Monahan, interview, October 7, 2010.

9. Ibid.

10. Roger Webb, interview, August 14, 2010.

11. Jim Guest, interview, August 31, 2010.

12. Pat Williams, interview, August 6, 2010; also, Jim Denney, *Coach Wooden: The 7 Principles That Shaped His Life and Will Change Yours* (Ada, MI: Baker Publishing Group/Revel Books, 2011).

13. Williams, interview.

14. Webb, interview.

15. Ibid.

16. Goldsmith, interview.

17. Ibid.

18. John Maxwell, interview, August 10, 2010.

19. Goldsmith, interview.

20. Ibid.; also, Kurt Eichenwald, *Conspiracy of Fools* (New York: Broadway Books, 2005).

21. Tammy Erickson, interview, August 30, 2010.

22. Reed, interview.

23. Ibid.

24. Vineet Nayar, interview, September 21, 2010.

25. Ibid.

26. Ibid.

Chapter 3

1. Terry Gross, "Horton Foote, Scripting Across the Ages," *Fresh Air,* National Public Radio broadcast, July, 8, 1988, rebroadcast March 12, 2009.

2. Dan Denison, interview, August 3, 2010.

3. C. K. Prahalad, born in India and recipient of a Ph.D. from Harvard, was a bestselling author and professor of strategy at the University of Michigan's Ross School of Business. He helped companies focus on core competencies and challenged companies to find ways to serve customers at "the bottom of the pyramid." See businessweek.com/magazine/content/10_18/b4176020893376.htm.

4. Denison, interview.

5. John Maxwell, interview, August 10, 2010.

6. Ibid.

7. Tom Draude, interview, August 27, 2010.

8. Ibid.

9. Michael Useem, interview, August 13, 2010.

10. Vineet Nayar, interview, September 21, 2010.

11. Ibid.

12. Ibid.

13. Ibid.

14. Ibid.

15. Useem, interview.

16. Ibid.

17. George Reed, interview, September 28, 2010.

18. Ibid.

19. Michelle Rhee, interview, August 3, 2010.

20. Ibid.

21. Tammy Erickson, interview, August 30, 2010.

22. Ibid.

23. Tom Monahan, interview, October 7, 2010.

24. Ibid.

25. Ibid.

26. Nayar, interview.

27. Jim Guest, interview, August 31, 2010.

28. Marshall Goldsmith, interview, August 14, 2010.

29. Roger Webb, interview, August 14, 2010.

30. Goldsmith, interview.

31. Franklin Roosevelt, address written for Jefferson Day, April 13, 1945, broadcast.

32. Franklin Roosevelt, Address, Oglethorpe University, May 22, 1932.

33. Pat Williams, interview, August 6, 2010.

Chapter 4

1. Sam Hill and Glenn Rifkin, *Radical Marketing* (New York: Harper Business, 1999), pp. 225–47; David Kesmodel, "Revolutionizing American Beer," *Wall Street Journal,* April 19, 2010; Jamie Allen, "Sam Adams Brewer: Jim Koch: Beer Career," *CNN.com,* March 16, 2001.

2. Kesmodel, "Revolutionizing."

3. John Maxwell, interview, August 10, 2010.

4. James C. Collins and Jerry I. Porras, *Built to Last* (New York: Harper-Business, 1994) p. 78.

5. John Baldoni, *How Great Leaders Get Great Results* (New York: McGraw-Hill, 2006).

6. Maxwell, interview.

7. Dan Denison, interview, August 3, 2010.

8. Ibid.

9. Tammy Erickson, interview, August 30, 2010.

10. Right Management 209 study, as cited in *Training* magazine, train-ingmag.com/msg/content_display/publications/e3ifcc0b6f995bc3974 edfe30b7c29b2d14.

11. Marshall Goldsmith, interview, August 14, 2010.

12. Goldsmith, interview; Marshall Goldsmith with Mark Reiter, *MOJO: How to Get It, How to Keep It, How to Get It Back if You Lose It* (New York: Hyperion, 2010).

13. Paul Spiegelman, interview, August 31, 2010.

14. Ibid.

Chapter 5

1. Emily Langer and T. Rees Shapiro, "Former Rep. Charlie Wilson Dies; Led U.S. Support of Afghans Against Soviets," *Washington Post,* February 11, 2010; "Charlie Wilson," *The Economist,* February 20, 2010; Douglas Wilson, "Charlie Wilson, Texas Congressman Linked to Foreign Intrigue, Dies at 76," *New York Times,* February 11, 2010. See also *Charlie Wilson's War,* film directed by Mike Nichols and written by Aaron Sorkin, based on *Charlie Wilson's War* by George Crile (New York: Grove Press, 2007).

2. Dwight Eisenhower, quoted in Richard Nixon, *Six Crises* (New York: Doubleday, 1962).

3. Dan Denison, interview, August 3, 2010; David Robertson, Ph.D., teaches innovation and IT management at the Wharton School at the University of Pennsylvania.

4. Denison, interview.

5. Michael Useem, interview, August 13, 2010.

6. Tom Monahan, interview, October 7, 2010.

7. Ibid.

8. Ibid.

9. Nancy Schlichting, interview, September 8, 2010.

10. Ibid.

11. Useem, interview.

12. Ibid.

13. Ibid.

14. Jim Guest, interview, August 31, 2010.

15. Denison, interview.

16. Marshall Goldsmith, interview, August 14, 2010.

17. Tom Draude, interview, August 27, 2010.

18. Ibid.

19. John Maxwell, interview, August 10, 2010.

20. Ibid.

21. Ibid.

22. George Reed, interview, September 28, 2010.

23. Schlichting, interview.

24. Ibid.

25. Ibid.

26. Paul Spiegelman, interview, August 31, 2010.

27. Ibid.

28. Ibid.

29. Ibid.

30. Reed, interview.

31. Tammy Erickson, interview, August 30, 2010.

32. Ibid.

33. Ibid.

34. Roger Webb, interview, August 14, 2010.

35. Ibid.

36. Nancy Austin is a popular keynote speaker and is the coauthor (with Tom Peters) of bestseller *A Passion for Excellence* (New York: Random House, 1985) and (with Stanlee Phelps) *The Assertive Woman* (New York: Impact, 2002); see also http://en.wikipedia.org/wiki/Nancy_Austin.

37. Alex Osborn coined the term "brainstorming."

Chapter 6

1. Frank Litsky and John Branch, "John Wooden, Who Built Incomparable Dynasty at UCLA, Dies at 99," *New York Times*, June 5, 2010; Jim Murray, "Wooden: The Greatest at Modesty, Too," *Los Angeles Times*, August 10, 1972.

2. Marshall Goldsmith, *Succession: Are You Ready?* (Boston: Harvard Business Press, 2009).

3. Marshall Goldsmith, interview, August 14, 2010.

4. Ibid.

5. See patwilliamsmotivate.com.

6. Pat Williams, interview, August 6, 2010.

7. Ibid.

8. Ibid.

9. Ibid.

10. John Maxwell, interview, August 10, 2010.

11. Michael Useem, interview, August 13, 2010.

12. Ibid.

13. Ibid.

14. Michelle Rhee, interview, August 3, 2010.

15. Ibid.

16. "Top 20 Companies for Leadership Development," *Bloomberg/ BusinessWeek*, February 16, 2010, businessweek.com/careers/ special_reports/20100216best_companies_for_leadership.htm.

17. Jim Guest, interview, August 31, 2010.

18. Tom Monahan, interview, October 7, 2010.

19. Ibid.

20. Ibid.

21. Ibid.

22. Paul Spiegelman, interview, August 31, 2010.

23. George Reed, interview, September 28, 2010.

24. Ram Charan, Stephen Drotter, and James Noel, *The Leadership Pipeline: How to Build the Leadership Powered Company* (New York: Jossey-Bass, 2000).

25. Reed, interview.

26. Ibid.

27. Ibid.

28. Spiegelman, interview.

29. Tom Draude, interview, August 27, 2010.

30. Ibid.

31. Nancy Schlichting, interview, September 8, 2010.

32. Tammy Erickson, interview, August 30, 2010.

33. Draude, interview.

34. Ibid.

35. Ibid.

Chapter 7

1. David Hackett Fischer, *Washington's Crossing* (New York: Oxford University Press, 2004); also, *American Heritage* 50, no. 4 (Winter 2010).

2. Ibid, *Washington's Crossing*.

3. Dave Davies, "Meet Lisa Sanders, the Doctor Behind 'House,'" *Fresh Air*, NPR broadcast, August 10, 2009, npr.org/templates/story/story .php?storyId = 111844063; Dr. Sanders also contributes columns on health to the *New York Times*.

4. Douglas Brinkley, *Wheels for the World: Henry Ford, His Company, and a Century of Progress* (New York: Viking, 2003), pp. 36, 69, citing Clifton Fadiman, ed., *The Little, Brown Book of Anecdotes* (Boston: Little, Brown, 1985), p. 213.

5. Definition of "negative capability" from letter to George and Thomas Keats, December 22, 1817.

6. Michael Useem, *The Go Point* (New York: Crown Business/Random House, 2006).

7. Robert Guth, "In a Secret Hideaway, Bill Gates Ponders Microsoft's Future," *Wall Street Journal*, March 28, 2005, online.wsj.com/ article_email/SB111196625830690477-IZjgYNklaB4o52sbHmIa 62Im4.html.

8. Gordon R. Sullivan and Michael V. Harper, *Hope Is Not the Method* (New York: Broadway Books, 1996).

9. John Baldoni, "When the Red Phone Rings, Three Questions to Ask in a Crisis," *Harvard Business Review*, March 10, 2008, http://blogs .harvardbusiness.org/cs/2008/03/when_the_red_phone_rings_three .html.

10. John Baldoni, "Detroit's Failure and How Not to Treat Employees," *Harvard Business Review*, December 12, 2008, http://blogs.harvard business.org/baldoni/2008/12/leadership_begins_with_honesty.html.

11. Dave Davies, "Re-Examining the Father of Modern Surgery," *Fresh Air*, NPR broadcast, February 22, 2010, npr.org/templates/story/story.php?storyId= 123570287.

12. Gerald Imber, *Genius on the Edge: The Bizzare Double Life of Dr. William Stewart Halsted* (New York: Kaplan, 2010).

13. As cited in the movie *Invictus*, and based on the book (see Chapter 2, note 2).

Action Planner

1. Abraham Lincoln, First Inaugural Address, Washington, D.C., March 4, 1861.

2. Victor Davis Hanson, *The Soul of Battle: From Ancient Times to the Present Day, How Three Great Liberators Vanquished Tyranny* (New York: Free Press, 1999).

3. John Baldoni, "A Better Kind of Leadership," December 19, 2007, FastCompany.com.

4. The American version of *The Office*, Reveille Productions/NBC Universal Productions, was adapted by Gred Daniels from the BBC series of the same name, created by Ricky Gervais and Stephen Merchant. It began running on NBC in 2005.

5. Terry Gross, interview with Steve Carell, *Fresh Air*, NPR broadcast, October 24, 2007.

6. Ibid.

7. John Baldoni, "Tune In or Forget It," October 31, 2007, FastCompany.com.

8. Nic Paton, "CEOs Worried by New Generation of Managers," October 5, 2007, management-issues.com; "U.S. Suffering a Critical Shortage of Middle Managers," May 17, 2007, management-issues .com.

9. Paton, "U.S. Suffering."

10. Phred Dvorak, "In the Lead: A Different Animal Seeks the No. 1 Job; Often, It's Not No. 2," *Wall Street Journal,* October 22, 2007.

11. John Baldoni, "Watch for the Reaction," November 7, 2007, Fast Company.com.

12. Aaron DeSmet, Monica McGurt, and Mark Vinson, "Unlocking the Potential of Front-Line Managers," *McKinsey Quarterly,* August 2009, mckinseyquarterly.com/Organization/Talent/Unlocking_the_ potential_of_frontline_managers_2418?gp = 1.

13. Ibid.

14. "Physiognomy and Success: Face Value," *The Economist,* January 26, 2008, socionix.com/vi/Facing%20Faces-Studies%20on%20the%20 Cognitive%20A spects%20of%2 0Physiognomy.pdf.

15. Alan Brinkley, *The Publisher: Henry Luce and the American Century* (New York: Knopf, 2010), pp. 267–71, 417–21.

16. "The American Century," *Life* magazine, February 7, 1941.

17. David Brooks, "Rush to Therapy," *New York Times,* November 9, 2009.

18. John Baldoni, "Craft a Narrative to Instill Optimism," *Harvard Business Review,* December 17, 2009, http://blogs.hbr.org/baldoni/ 2009/12/craft_a_narrative_to_instil.html.

19. E. B. White, *Stuart Little* (New York: HarperTrophy, 1945).

INDEX

ABOUT THE AUTHOR

John Baldoni is an internationally recognized leadership educator, executive coach, and author of many books, including *Lead by Example, Lead Your Boss,* and *Great Motivation Secrets of Great Leaders.* John is much in demand as a speaker, and in 2011, Leadership Gurus International ranked him No. 11 on its list of top 30 global leadership experts. John is a regular online contributor to *Harvard Business Review* and *Bloomberg/Businessweek.* His leadership resource website is www.john baldoni.com.